THE SURROUNDS

Theory in Forms | A series edited by Nancy Rose Hunt and Achille Mbembe

URBAN
LIFE
WITHIN AND
BEYOND CAPTURE

THE

SURROUNDS

ABDOUMALIQ
SIMONE

Duke University Press   Durham and London   2022

publication supported by a grant from
The Community Foundation for Greater New Haven
as part of the **Urban Haven Project**

Designed by Aimee C. Harrison
Typeset in Garamond Premier Pro and Helvetica Neue by
Westchester Publishing Services

Library of Congress Cataloging-in-Publication Data
Names: Simone, A. M. (Abdou Maliqalim), [date] author.
Title: The surrounds : urban life within and beyond capture /
AbdouMaliq Simone.
Other titles: Theory in forms.
Description: Durham : Duke University Press, 2022. | Series: Theory
in forms | Includes bibliographical references and index. Identifiers:
LCCN 2021033422 (print)
LCCN 2021033423 (ebook)
ISBN 9781478015505 (hardcover)
ISBN 9781478018131 (paperback)
ISBN 9781478022749 (ebook)
Subjects: LCSH: Urbanization—Developing countries. | Sociology,
Urban—Developing countries. | Human geography—Developing
countries. | Social ecology—Developing countries. | Marginality,
Social—Developing countries. | Decolonization—Developing
countries. | BISAC: SOCIAL SCIENCE / Sociology / Urban | SOCIAL
SCIENCE / Human Geography
Classification: LCC HT149.5.s57 2022 (print) | LCC HT149.5 (ebook) |
DDC 307.76—dc23/eng/20211015
LC record available at https://lccn.loc.gov/2021033422
LC ebook record available at https://lccn.loc.gov/2021033423

Cover art: Raqs Media Collective, still from *Strikes at Time*,
2011. Courtesy of Raqs Media Collective and Frith Street
Gallery, London.

Contents

Preface

This monograph on the surrounds is based on a series of three lectures delivered under the auspices of the Sheffield Urbanism Lecture Series, October–November 2020. These lectures were titled "From Extinction to Abolition" and attempted to explore the ways in which both extinction and abolition are prefigured within diverse urban environments, and how what presents itself as dissipative and useless often conceals a site of potential generativity, of transversals that point to improbable yet existent responses to persistent injustice. These lectures were primarily rehearsals for a range of different conceptualizations and ways of bringing together diverse theoretical and field materials not under any overarching rubric but as a gathering of the disparate, an attempt to narrate how they might find their way to and through each other. This book builds on these rehearsals, developing an architecture of loose ligatures that can hold these rehearsals together as a sustained commentary on *extensive* urbanization. Here, *extensive* does not mean the extending across space of a univocal process of urbanization. Rather, *extensive* refers to how the growth of the urban, in its appropriations of and extractions from heterogeneous logics, practices, and modes of accumulation, extends the urban beyond either the clearly recognizable forms or the spaces that are subsumed to specific operations or values (Mezzadra 2019). Thus, the surrounds.

This Sheffield series followed three lectures offered at the University of Cambridge in November 2017. Those initial lectures centered around the notion of the *uninhabitable*. Building on reflections of Katherine McKittrick (2006), this notion does not so much concern those aspects of urban life that made human residency, for some, nearly impossible but instead seeks to identify those aspects of urbanization that do not fundamentally center on or concern the possibilities of inhabitation. That is, even though urbanization is driven by human activity, it entails intersections of materials, things, and times that assume unanticipated dispositions, that produce eventfulness and potentialities that do not so much foreclose residency as continuously shift what it means to reside, what it means to instantiate a sense of home or position.

The *uninhabitable* also refers to collective lives of continuous remaking, where the rootedness of a sense of "we" within territorial emplacement and identification both exceeds these parameters and continuously posits new intersections among the ways in which the material operations of urban space are composed. These are new intersections between the abstract designs that steer such operations and the collective enunciations that make sense of them. These formulations on the uninhabitable are ways of seeing how specific urbanization processes constitute what Michel Foucault (1986) called the ungrounded arts of existence—those practices and desires that are aimed neither at furthering life, nor at institutionalizing settled forms of recognition.

In the subsequent book derived from these initial lectures, *Improvised Lives: Rhythms of Endurance in an Urban South*, logics of what has often been referred to as "Great Black Music" (rather than jazz) were mobilized to examine how ensemble work constitutes a particularly salient mode or metaphor for navigating terrains of the uninhabitable. Rather than focus on the conventional tropes of political mobilization or collectivities rooted in accordance with clearly delineated identities or territories of belonging, ensemble work constituted a convergence of disparate technicities and soundings capable of playing the same "notes," the same "score," but generating entirely different trajectories of sonic possibility. The attempt was to extend this notion to the ways in which the continuous reinvention of capital across "Global Southern latitudes" was, in the end, driven by changing ensembles of the marginal:

> In a game of state politics, where affordances and territory are continuously reapportioned to different factions, where the overconfidence of big developers and real estate financiers is increasingly punctuated by an incessant anxiety of getting the timing right, of having to preside over intricate sutures of money, land, labor, technology, rules and political deals, maintaining peripheries as spaces of compressed livelihoods, maneuvers, and backgrounds is critical. They not only offer a possible hedge against the bulldozing regimens of homogenizing shopping malls, industrial parks and export-processing zones, but are also instruments of leverage within that very game. (Simone 2018, 135–36)

This present book extends these notions through the invocation of *the surrounds* as simultaneously the spaces, times, and practices within and beyond capture, where experiences of detachment from the predominant forms of accumulation and dispossession enable the specification of dispositions in ways that ward off being apprehended in any definitive sense—where moments of suspension from the traumas and obligations occasioned by individual and collective memory are momentarily possible. The surrounds can function as a literal type of territorialization possible when extensive and extended urbanization is no longer rooted within the *city form*, and thus dependent upon multiple articulations of different ways of doing things and different logics of settlement and production. These are, in turn, sutured together, not through a single overarching process but rather through a range of plural stitching and mutual implication.

Acknowledgments

This project could not have been completed without the generous support of my colleagues at the Urban Institute, University of Sheffield: Simon Marvin, Beth Perry, Aidan While, Vanesa Castán Broto, and Jonathan Silver. The "Gang of Four," with Teresa Caldeira, Kelly Gillespie, and Gautam Bhan has over the years provided the essential friendship, care, and intellectual inspiration through ongoing collective thinking and writing. The book is also indebted to the support, guidance, and reflections of my most important interlocutors and comrades: Edgar Pieterse, Anant Maringanti, Miya Irawati, Tanya Chandra, Michael Keith, Ryan Bishop, Filip de Boeck, Laura Kemmer, Sabine Mohamed, Dian Tri, Marco Kusumawijaya, Verónica Gago, Cristina Ceilo, Tau Tavengwa, Prasad Shetty, Solomon Benjamin, Vyjayanthi Rao, Lisa Damon, Morten Nielsen, Pernille Barnhëim, and Iremelin Joelsson.

Finally, this project could never have been completed without the everyday intellectual, affective, and logistical support of my brother, Michele Lancione, and my partner in research and everything else, Rika Febriyani.

INTRODUCTION

EXPOSING
THE SURROUNDS
AS URBAN
INFRASTRUCTURE

Going Around

In spring 2020, global media was captivated by images of Indian urban migrant workers walking home, often thousands of kilometers away (*Times of
India* 2020). The pandemic-induced lockdowns put at least a temporary end
to their already precarious jobs, jobs that left little opportunity to acquire
any kind of savings, jobs that barely covered the costs of a bed in a hostel
and a single meal a day. Existing as the cheapest labor possible, thoroughly
expendable and ineligible for other opportunities in these cities, these workers were left little choice but to return to homes most had not visited in years.

Many NGOs and community associations were mobilized to provide
transportation and food for these migrant workers on their way "home." This
included my colleagues at the Hyderabad Urban Lab (HUL), who were constantly on the phone with local councilors, businesspersons, and social welfare agencies in an effort to organize a coordinated response in Hyderabad.
Unlike many organizations that viewed the situation only as a problem to
be solved, HUL made a concerted effort to elicit stories from departing migrants regarding their past employment conditions, hopes, and aspirations.

It tried to find ways of interlinking these stories in narratives that sought to understand the characteristics of the social lives that these migrants had attempted to piece together with each other and the ways in which these lives not only were fractured by the closing of factories and the imposition of pandemic controls but now were being extended across different geographies. In these collected stories, it isn't so much that home was seen as the place of any stability, of any strong affective attachment. Rather, many of those heading across the scorching highways indicated that it was simply a place from which to think, to assess, to contemplate the next move. These workers would not necessarily return to the cities from which they were departing, but they also didn't expect to remain long in those places to which they were going.

Drawing much less attention than those workers on their way "home," HUL also encountered other workers who neither stayed where they were nor left. Although some were indeed immobilized from the sheer uncertainty of their situations, there were other workers who simply set off from their hostels, their entanglement in improvised relations of care, debt, making do, and exploitation, and headed somewhere, seemingly without a plan, without clear direction. When my colleagues at HUL attempted to find out more about these workers' choices, some simply stated, "We have more work to do." So the question is, what is this work? Long seen as simply bodies who labor, and labor at the most menial and backbreaking jobs, this invocation of having more work to do points to a refusal to be reduced to labor. While most workers HUL engaged were leaving the city to find some kind of exteriority from which to reassess the prospects for their lives, those workers who remained were telling HUL something else, something about how their position within Hyderabad was always already something more than sheer labor, that there was something about this position that required work beyond the factory and hostel, and now that, for the moment, they were dismissed from factories and hostels, this "other work" was to be done with all seriousness. They sought to find within the city those spaces of operation that perhaps only they could identify and elaborate.

Some would describe this journey as a matter of paying attention to the slightest details: the color of a rusting truck seemingly unmoved for generations; the sudden and inexplicable laughter of crowds of women hurrying home after some essential but now furtive shopping; the flickers of neon lighting emanating from an empty schoolyard. These details operated as indecipherable signs yet were operationalized as directions—time to go left and down this road, or time to stop and take momentary shelter in the hollowed-out confines of an abandoned building's parking garage. Across

2

these improvised and arbitrary itineraries, there were sufficient numbers of public soup kitchens to be visited, and of course, things always fall off trucks and unanticipated generosities sometimes manifest. The twelve- to sixteen-hour shifts these workers had usually put in had acted as a kind of confinement; they rarely had opportunities to take in the larger city in which they were embedded.

Without commitments or attachments, without the luxury to compare themselves to others, and refusing the obligation always to think of the others to whom they had been attached, these excursions revealed all varieties of spaces that didn't seem to be committed or attached to the uses they would seem to purport. This was not only a matter of schools being turned into vast communal houses, markets into mathematics classrooms for orphaned teenagers, shrines into all-night popular political assemblies, or government tax offices into repair shops for homemade inventions. Rather, these were all those spaces in the midst of things, within crowded thoroughfares, jetties, underpasses, hallways, and arenas that didn't quite fit with what was happening around them. Spaces ever so slightly out of joint, where the anomalous, the marginal, while clearly visible, remained ever so slightly undetectable, enough for moments of rest, the rehearsing of some kind of weirdness, a base from which to build a modicum of confidence to venture forward or back.

It wasn't that these excursions were going to lead to any salvation or posit a new horizon of opportunity and security. It wasn't that these workers who remained garnered any clear sense of what they needed to do or could do. But almost all of them, without fail, indicated a renewed determination to stay, not as they were but as something else. They talked about a newfound ability to ask questions of strangers, to deliver the necessary niceties and ingratiation to make somewhat outlandish propositions as a way of registering the elasticity of particular personalities and situations. They talked about how they would acquire random partners who accompanied them part of the way and that these companions would ask them questions about things they had never considered or at least had not deemed themselves sufficiently worthy to consider. Something was taking shape. They couldn't always hold onto what it was, and they would have to start over again, but none reported this as a traumatic loss or a foregone conclusion. Of course, incessant movement is wearying, and the indeterminacy of purpose and result is difficult to sustain. At the same time, they felt less marginal to the city, they sensed that they surrounded all that they traversed with something that did not exist there before. They sensed that even though they were not essential workers, they were an essential surrounds.

What Is/Are the Surrounds?

Instead of envisioning processes of urbanization as the unfolding of definitive forces of value capture, asset creation, and resource extraction, one must ask how these salient categorizations of spatial production are accompanied by a growing multiplicity of entities and their exertions. Particularly at the extensions, just beyond what has customarily been purported to be the "real city," it is increasingly evident that a continuous recalibration of "projects," material inputs and residues, and altered ecologies of reciprocal causation are generating landscapes that exceed the salience of available vernaculars of analysis and intervention. Here, intricate landscapes of provisional sutures, half-lives, diffractions, disjuncture, compensation, and transience create unsettled urbanities and populations.

While dedicated genealogies may be capable of grasping how particular built environments, spatial dispositions, and fabrics got to be the way they manifest themselves, there is something that eludes coherent narratives of development and prospective futures. These are spaces of intensive contiguity of the disparate—disparate forms, functions, and ways of doing things. Such spaces are replete with gaps, interstices, breakdowns, contested territories, and sediments of dissonant tenure regimes, financing, legalities, and use. Instead of being able to discern legible articulations among the details of composition, these proliferations of housing, commercial, industrial, logistical, recreational, entrepreneurial, and governmental projects are less subsumed into overarching logics of capital accumulation or neoliberal rationalities than they are "strange accompaniments" to each other. Nothing quite fits according to design. Things dissipate or endure without obvious reason, and improvised alliances of use and rule continuously reshape what it is possible for any particular individual or institutional actor to do.

While now perhaps most evident at the extensions, these spatial formations of the disparate do not occur only within these extensions. Rather, they proliferate across all kinds of urban geographies. As such, the consideration of these disparate forms is not just a matter of space but one of time, of things coming and going, appearing and disappearing and reappearing again, dependent on the practices through which they are engaged.

I call this mode of accompaniment, of not clearly discernible or translatable territories of operation, *the surrounds*. The surrounds constitute neither an explanatory context nor a relation of interdependency. They are neither a strictly geographical nor a temporal phenomenon but can alternate to varying degrees. The surrounds do not surround a given space, project, environment,

Intro.1 | Extensions of Jakarta. Photograph by the author.

or ecology as a boundary limit or as some constitutive outside. They are not some alternate reality, just over there, just beyond the tracks or the near horizon. Sometimes they are heterotopic, exceptional, intensely specific, hidden in plain sight, prefigurative, or dissolute. In all instances the surrounds are infrastructural in that they entail the possibilities within any event, situation, setting, or project for something incomputable and unanticipated to take (its) place.

At the outset there is the question of whether the surrounds are singular or heterogeneously plural. Is it one kind of thing or many? The answer throughout this text is that they are somewhere in between or, in Marilyn Strathern's (1991, 27) formulation, "more than one and less than many." The surrounds can take the form of an untranslatable specificity but yet remain always in the form of the multiple, of many specificities, and thus not simply reducible to "one thing." The fact that the surrounds then "show up" across different contexts in many different forms renders them a prolific possibility, capable of appearing across many different kinds of structural constraints but without having to demonstrate a set of common features. At the same time, this multiplication of specificity needs some kind of connective tissue, some kind of at least vague assurance that each instantiation is not simply an anomaly, exception, or transgression, that each participates in something

5

beyond itself, and thus the surrounds comes to act as a concept or as a possibility inherent in the very formations of urban life. As a marker of this in-between position, while encumbered by the linguistic constraints of indicating the one or the many, reference will be made to surrounds across these shifting registers, highlighting at times the dimensions of singularity and at other times that connective tissue pointed to earlier.

In each sense, singular and plural, the surrounds is a product of a *relational location* rather than a geographic one. Cities are replete with clearly designated spaces—industrial, carceral, administrative, domestic, festive, logistical. But there is always something "left over" in their operations, something not completely captured by the terms of their respective functioning. Then there are spaces that seem to comprise elements of all these functions; spaces that are partly carceral, domestic, administrative, and so forth, but where the proportions of each characteristic are too difficult to discern or to stabilize within any particular calculation. Just as soon as you think you know what they are, they "move on," or the function on which you have staked your analysis is suddenly superseded by others. So the surrounds is the relationship among spaces, whose complexion exceeds their function while maintaining them and whose functions are never clearly stabilized because they seem to absorb the multiplicity of characteristics that makes up the place of the surrounds. Each of these distinct circumstances surrounds the other. Not necessarily liminal zones, terroir vague, secret recesses, or domains of uncertainty, each space is in most circumstances clearly identifiable, accessible, with little reticence about announcing itself. But in this relationship between what exceeds definition and coherence and what insufficiently consolidates clear definition is an interstice of momentary possibility: a possibility for propositions and the rehearsal of experimental ways of living that circumvent debilitating extraction, surveillance, and capture—for the time being.

Forms of the urban are engendered across different registers and scales, whereby the elaboration of proficient logistical systems, modes of computation and interoperability, obdurate practices of long-honed livelihoods, financialization, and makeshift economies coincide, exerting a specific agency, albeit in disproportionate capacities. As indicated earlier, it is particularly in the figurative surrounds of the city, those arenas in which urbanization is being extended and, in turn, extending these processes in multiple and sometimes unprecedented ways, in which it is possible to amplify the existence of a more conceptual surrounds as a relational location, one that also entails a different kind of time. This surrounds is a tremulous, provisional interstice among disparate forms of spatial development that often concretely sit right

Intro.2 | Young man working within and beyond. Photograph by Michele Lancione.

next to each other, that physically overlap but do not touch completely, that do not have a *settled* relationship.

As such, the surrounds comes to embody a more generalized process of unsettlement, a maximizing of *exposures*, which like the apertures of cameras, fundamentally disturb the image of something that may have otherwise been taken as "for sure." Intensified exposure can be seen as representing the intense precarity of urban lives in the so-called Global South, as well as the compiling of indebtedness driven by promises of middle-class attainment through consumption and the subsequent disappointments as to what this consumption has really accomplished. For those to whom opportunities for indebtedness were never offered, who were forced to completely improvise their daily existence, the proliferation of games of chance, of dissimilitude, of working around the constraints or seizing the weakly guarded, was often enough to hold on to some kind of anchorage in the city. But these opportunities, too, are also shrinking, and the subsequent desperation is sometimes repurposed as a threat, an instrument of blackmail, even as such populations can now become, quite literally, expendable, as exemplified in the extrajudicial killings of Rodrigo Duterte's Philippines or by those workers forced to walk hundreds of kilometers to their homes. Exposed to intensified vulnerability and cruelty, they alternate between having little and having everything to lose.

7

Exposures to Accompaniment

Exposure also entails a more volitional suspension of settlement, an often impulsive but determined decision to upend valued ways of living and operating within specific spaces in favor of more provisional circulations through various sites, occupations, and household compositions. Here, there is a more opportunistic, speculative orientation to urban futures for which any systematic planning or preparation makes little sense. It is all about being in the right place at the right time. But that right time is not foreseeable in advance. Rather, it is the outcome of simply "being there." "Being there" in any particular emplacement is increasingly short-lived, as lengths of residential and work tenancies shrink. Youths in particular are more inclined to make impatient assessments about what a particular job, place, or training program has to offer. Increasing one's exposure to the various spaces and populations of the larger urban region assumes greater importance, with its concomitant sense that what is available within a particular place is simply not sufficient for the future that is coming.

So, urban residents are increasingly situated in multiple exposures. There is the exposure to environments shaped by forces seen as being beyond one's control. There is the exposure of wounds and trauma; the exposure of the insufficiency of any livelihood or political project to affect the array of forces that exceeds anyone's capacity to pay attention or understand. But there is also the practice of residents exposing themselves to more nebulous eventualities, a conviction that passing through different territories, deals, itineraries, games, and conversations somehow prefigures and culminates in a space that both absorbs the weight of exploitation and simultaneously detaches from it. I will return to this notion of exposure in chapter 2, when I talk about how many of my associates in Jakarta view exposure as a critical method of inhabitation.

Many residents of Jakarta, Phnom Penh, and Delhi with whom I have worked over the past fifteen years do not have any clear idea about exactly what is being prefigured or what kind of life is likely to work. As they increasingly cannot count on the familiar infrastructures of care or see these infrastructures as inadequate in preparing for an uncertain future, they "drag" them across the thresholds of various operations that are not clearly collective but neither are they individual. Families and friends are set in motion, encouraged to spread out across cities to hunt for momentary opportunities. It is not that a single opportunity will be construed as the most opportune or a final destination. The objective is to multiply opportunities, find ways in

8

which they complement each other; the endurance of households is staked more on individual members inserting themselves in various "elsewheres" than on consolidating themselves in place. The concomitant itineraries of circulation across urban regions for one person are *accompanied* by the itineraries of many others also in circulation. Together, they forge momentary tribes of scavengers, adventurers, mercenaries, and friends in movement. For many, home remains somewhere, is revisited time and time again, often simply as place of momentary parking but then vacated again.

For those households with even some limited savings or multiple incomes, home is distributed across multiple sites, each hedging on the eventual prospects of increased valuation or access to opportunities. Each outpost surrounds the other; it changes function depending on whether it is a place of refuge, a primary residence, a rental for additional income, or a place of storage or commerce—a continuous relay, back and forth, of shifting investments and assessments.

Particularly at the peripheries of urban regions—in the sense of the actual hinterlands and those domains, regardless of physical location, that remain or become marginal to the officially valorized components of an urban economy—layer upon layer of sedimentation of diverging tenure systems, land uses, and regulatory frameworks are never quite subsumed into an overarching authority. Megacomplexes sit next to active farmland, owned perhaps by large corporations to offset taxation. These sit next to thousands of units of migrant hostels, sit next to industrial parks, sit next to thousands of small pavilions of so-called affordable housing, sit next to artisanal workshops—all without settled relations to one another but rather in relations that produce gaps, uncontrolled or undersurveilled spaces. The spaces may indeed be *surrounded* by both an emergent order of rationalization that will come to settle present uncertainties and a sense that *eventually* what exists as unprofitable, over- or underbuilt, informal, or tacitly contested will be normatively valuable. But for the time being, such spaces become opportunities for rehearsal, for experiencing the possibility of being exposed to something unprecedented, caring, and suggestive of new ways of moving and living.

One might see the surrounds as a kind of urbanization from below, a materialization of a more pluriversal territorialization of urban space, or an essential subaltern politics. Indeed, there is much to suggest that the surrounds, as posited here, lines up with these conceptualizations. Certainly the propositions offered by Arturo Escobar (2019), Asef Bayat (2013), and Gautam Bhan (2019) have been instrumental to the propositions offered

9

Intro.3 | One thousand doors of Jakarta extensions. Photograph by Miya Irawati.

here. Rather than identify a particular scalar register or attribute capacity to a particular kind of actor or positionality, the surrounds here are suggested as a kind of accompaniment to processes underway from those different scales and actors. It is not a relationship of symbiosis, co-constitution, or codependency but of companionship not based on the recitation of complementary interests or reciprocities.

Neither the spatial products nor processes under consideration necessarily need a surrounds, so whether an accompaniment is present is a matter detached from the character of those products and processes. Accompaniment means something that operates aside, on the side, that does not entail obligation or a manifestation of mutual desire. If I accompany someone it does not mean that the person accompanied could not accomplish a designated task on their own. Someone can still perform "solo" without missing something essential. Accompaniment is a supplement that shows up, now and then, and goes along for the ride. It is not unaffected by the going along, but it is not essentially invested in the outcome of the task at hand. It does not constitute a debt owed the recipient, even though such debt might ensue from a particular accompaniment.

This book's intent, then, is to draw attention to the ways in which we are accompanied by an array of "companions" throughout the urban environment. Rather than seeing the built environment as the stage through which to exercise our privileges or as the concretization of aspirations, needs, and accomplishments, the built environment acts as an accompaniment to whatever we do. It pays attention to our practices; it bears witness to our travails and attainments. There is always something not used or only partially used, something that remains just out of reach, something barely noticeable or deemed irrelevant that accompanies all that is standard operating procedure, all the demarcated, sectored, and zoned spatial arrangements. Accompaniment is a submergent infrastructure that suggests something other than what is recognized.

Surrounds as Infrastructural Effect

For this reason, the surrounds here is considered a fundamental urban infrastructural effect.

As a method of formatting, of bringing form into existence and informing matter, infrastructure may seem to be informed by linear visions, clearly demarcated lines from "here" to "there," or a geometric arrangement of materials in space. But infrastructure also restitutes potentials that have been subtracted by subject-centered ways of seeing, which establish specific sensory boundaries and angles of relational possibilities delimiting what is relevant to an existence and what is not (Anand, Gupta, and Appel 2018). But infrastructure is never complete, neither in its closure to further articulations nor in its process of immediate decay. It may be repaired, expanded, and updated, and as such it constantly shows evidence of not only what it bears and extracts, or the force that it imparts, but the limits of its anticipations. For in trying to impose specific lines of connection, it implicitly excludes others that remain to haunt it, that simply do not get out of the way or cease acting just because the concrete is poured, the pipes laid, or the wires drawn. So if the surrounds are an infrastructural effect, they, too, carry with them an ambivalence of use, for they can be as much exploited and exhausted as they can enable indeterminate uses and endure.

Infrastructure can be read as the embodiment of specific instantiations of capital flows, the aspirations of various kinds of articulation, the concretization of political accords; as strategic devices for socializing bodies and places; and as technologies for *throwntogetherness* (Massey 2005, 94). Yet equally important, infrastructure can be seen as a gesture toward the uncertain stabilities that exist in and as a result of the territorialization of space into discernible points, units, tangents, and vectors. Instead of a constantly expansive hardwiring of metabolism, atmosphere, and geomorphology, infrastructure is also an increasingly frenetic signaling of volatility. Each suture, hinge, circumvention, or agglomeration is insufficient to the uncertainty infrastructure both registers and constitutes. Creative destruction makes infrastructure a plaything in the recalibration of value; exhaustion acts as a crisis that prompts repairs and renovation; and aesthetic incompatibility to prevailing sentiments subjects infrastructure to radical makeovers. But from its inception, infrastructure seems to point to the simultaneous presence of many temporalities—all the actions never quite constellated as event, all the intersections and transactions that either could have happened somewhere but didn't, or that did but didn't go anywhere specific or didn't leave enough of a tangible trace to point back to or move on from.

Environs are replete with what Brian Massumi (2014, 20–21) calls "bare activities," imperceptible adjustments and immediately lived hypotheses about what is about to happen that incline persons to attend to particular textures, pathways in the landscape at hand. A thickly configured affective field pulsates with tensions constantly worked out, usually under any radar or conscious deliberation. Infrastructure intervenes not only to constitute starting positions from which to trace webs of causation, relevance, and impact but also to etch out channels of evacuation. What is important is not only what infrastructure brings together, how it connects actions, bodies, and sites, but also how it provides channeled lines of flight that provide a way for people and things to get away from having to absorb or be the bearings of work, home, institution, or place. What might happen if we stayed on this bus route beyond our designated stop or failed to get off at this highway exit; what would happen if we walked through all those back alleys and hidden trails, or left the pavement or even the ground to wander across rooftops or subterranean tunnels? What would happen if we had master keys or security codes and passes to cut through gates and barriers?

Still, the primary trajectory of infrastructure seems to "run away" from the intense simultaneity of multiple temporalities—the prospect that many things could and did happen somewhere. So the burden of bearing the weight of such intensity is displaced through the connective tissue of infrastructures. Pass, move things on, even when so many things are so tightly brought together. Concentration becomes the possibility of dispersal, even when things seem to be so well held in place. From infrastructure we come to know what the vast multiplicity of activity taking place concurrently and incipiently means for us in terms of its likely impact on our lives. But we are also constantly reminded of what we don't know. Our everyday routines and itineraries constantly skirt on the interface between habituation and improvisation, where improvisation entails knowing from where we set off but also always raises that question about how to get "home."

Imagine how it is possible to leave your house and set off and keep going without having any destination in mind other than the next step. If you are sufficiently funded, you can keep going indefinitely. Without map, plan, or anticipation, the emerging itinerary becomes an entanglement of memory, impulse, desire, and calculation. To continue constantly without a destination in mind is the implicit premise of infrastructure. Even as it orders and structures discernible courses of action and conveyances of cause and effect, it also seems to set things loose, pointing to how turbulent whatever seems stable actually is. How to occupy this turbulence—for a person cannot live *in* turbulence for very long—is the challenge posed by the surrounds. It is a challenge of pacing and rhythm: how to slow things down sufficiently to have opportunities to practice new ways of doing things or recuperate lost and cherished methods but without habituating to the particularities of the locale or worrying about what can be retained and applied to the next occupation; to find in that short-lived moment the ability to be an accompaniment to others on their way.

Blackness as Urban Force

A critical objective of this book is also to find ways of incorporating the variegated corpus of contemporary Black critical thought as a resource to think through urbanization processes underway. This is not so much a reflection on ways in which various urban contexts treat Black residency or bend theorizations of the urban to consider the unacknowledged importance of blackness to the shaping of urban life. Rather, it is a reflection on ways to read the contemporary urban through the lens of such thought and to draw on the range of instruments of everyday practice and collective consciousness offered in specific formulations of the Black "social," "political," and "emancipatory" to identify spaces and times of the surrounds within the urban, particularly that of the Global South. Blackness here operates as method for experimental investigations, particularly aimed at the discovery of what *might be happening right now*, as specific propositions or prefiguring the abolition of not only the predicates of the carceral but also the urban reality as we know it.

It is important to emphasize that this is an exploratory, tentative deployment of Black thought to a project I have characterized as incumbent on residents themselves. For many with whom I have worked and lived in Jakarta, there are always new attempts to bring the discrepant into momentary constellations of investigation, to look at things through new angles, to explore new terrain. It is an intensely restless city, and moving around is time consuming and often produces few rewards. But there is an increasingly widespread recognition that one takes wherever one is at the moment as a launching pad into something else. For what is to come is something that is being *prefigured* through one's very movements among different sets of contacts, temporary shelters, and improvised gatherings. My fellow residents look for suggestions, not definitions; they look to be pointed in directions they cannot yet see. So, too, in this book, the deployment of select strands of Black intellectual and political work is suggestive, heuristic. It is not interested in coherently defining a "Black contribution" and, as such, will "get things wrong." It may be impervious to the intricate architectures of thought and experience that have informed critical Black thought for generations. Who I am means that I will inevitably get things wrong, but the book seeks to live with this insufficiency while not being deterred from trying things out, given that countering the precarity and marginality of so many particularly Southern urban spaces and practices is now urgent.

As the subtitle of the Sheffield lectures cited in the preface, "From Extinction to Abolition," suggests, the concern was (and is) to reconsider abolition's essential proposition—*the changing of everything*—as a focus of a heuristic urban ethnography of *what has already been completely changed* even as the conditions for empirically verifying such transformation are not presently possible. This ethnography is not just a phantasmagoric redescription accomplished through an inventive poetics (although it is partially that). Rather, it is a way of thinking *incipience* not simply as sign of what is to become or could become but as an actual experience of unsettling, a moment of diffracted sense, where things could go many different ways, where life at the moment is staked on *the maybe*—where every available means of calculation goes no further than "maybe it will, or maybe it won't." At that moment, in that space, there is nothing beyond the *maybe*. This is where a sense of proportion breaks down; where it is not possible to tell what is one's own calculation, what is some diffuse *call* from somewhere beckoning one forward, or what is pure chance or fate.

From extinction to abolition does not then mark a definitive trajectory or process. After all, extinction would change everything too, leaving nothing in its wake. In a limited sense the "from" indicates how the prospect of human disappearance is wrapped up in the way in which the very proposition of the human has been contingent on assigning specific bodies and lives to the categories outside the human or as the antithesis of the human. The "from" indicates the ways in which the prospects of unsustained human life can be directly attributed to the maneuver of dismissal and exclusion, and it indicates that any prospects for endurance require the abolition of that fundamental relation.

What I emphasize in this book is a sense that thinking through an already extant extinction, an exploration of spaces and times where the human is simply not regarded as present or particularly significant may be part and parcel of identifying a surrounds—in the sense of a space beyond capture within capture. Again, authors such as Katherine McKittrick (2013, 2021), Neferti X. M. Tadiar (2022), Tiffany Lethabo King (2019), Deborah Thomas (2019), and Sylvia Wynter (2003) have all written about spaces that have operated as a surrounds to specific sites and historical periods, and their work has been absolutely critical to the formulations offered here. Long histories of grand marronage are also salient here because they point to the ongoing conundrum entailed in moving from confinement to freedom. The flight from captivity was not only an attempt to extricate oneself from the plantation system but a means to unsettle its hegemony, to demonstrate the viability of possible outsides. Yet, any unsettling had to be complemented by the exigencies and practicalities of resettling.

At times, the destinations involved could attain a measure of self-sufficiency, settlements outside the scope of retribution or recapture. But many maroon communities could be established only in territories that necessitated being folded, at least partially, into the sovereignty of that plantation system. This could take the form of regulating the mobility of new generations of runaway slaves or indentured workers or of serving as a supplementary force intervening in internecine conflicts among disparate colonial interests. At still other times, marronage took the form of partial incorporation into other groups that existed at the margins of colonial regimes, such as one of the various indigenous groups often occupying seemingly uninhabitable terrain, which also limited the mobility and maneuverability of the maroon (Diouf 2014; Roberts 2015). Whatever the disposition, this transition "from" indicates the dilemmas of a fugitivity, where sometimes there were simply no places to run to, to hide at, to begin anew from, or if there were, they were often situated within inhospitable terrain, problematic partial connections to that which was left behind. All necessitated various ways of becoming imperceptible (Deleuze and Guattari 2013).

Urban Matters

Throughout this book, my concern is exclusively *urban*. I do not intend to weigh in on contemporary theorizations or political struggles about abolition. Rather the objective is to consider how abolitionist ontologies are inscribed in the very extensivity of urbanization. Even in the interest of continuous accumulation and extraction of surplus value, the extension of the urban entails offering a particular working out of dilemmas faced by human settlements. This working out entails various equations of subsumption, adaptation, erasure, remaking, conciliation, and improvisation. Urbanization is not only something that spreads out as a function of its own internal operations but something that is contributed to through an intensely differentiated process of encounter that enables it to change gears and operate through a wider range of appearances and instantiations. If urbanization is extensive, it is so not only in the sense that it covers more ground or becomes an increasingly hegemonic modality of spatial and social production but also in the sense that it "shows up" as a key facet in the operations of institutions and sectors not previously considered urban.

These encounters, beyond simple metaphors of algorithmic combination, entail a fundamental aspect of the incomputable, or what Luciana Parisi (2013, 92) calls "incompressible data." It concerns how dispositions veer off into something unintelligible, or ungraspable, with the available interpretive tools. If urbanization is not then simply the rollout of some overarching macroeconomic dynamic or the operations of the axiomatics of capital, it is also replete with rhythms of articulation that stutter, that act as if possessed by some divinatory force, that veer off only to reverberate somewhere unexpected. This book, then, is an attempted geography of those rhythms, apertures, detours, and interstitial layerings that seem to come from nowhere, that might appear as exceptions, exemptions, or eventually incorporable singularities but that are "coded" into the very propulsion of the urban itself.

In many respects the narrative voice here is conversational. I make frequent use of a generic "we"—for example, "we face this"; this is "our situation." Who is the "we" here? Because this is an urban book, I am addressing urban residents, as if, in terms of prevailing conditions, "we are all in this together." And "we" know well that "we" are not; that the urban is the embodiment of difference and the machinic production of difference, and that the characteristics of those differences are different themselves. They are a constant recalibration of whose lives count for what; who can be used and acknowledged for what. Residents are always situated within the urban differently, and those differences are made to count in ways that exceed the desires and controls of those who bear them.

Adam Bledsoe and Willie Wright (2018) emphasize the ways in which Black geographies are rendered *aspatial*—incapable of acquiring genealogical substantiation, continuous and incremental histories of development—as a way of making them available to new projects of capital accumulation and extraction, as if nothing happens in those spaces. Urban residency knows no common default position, and here Black inhabitation amplifies the need to pay attention to how urban spaces are actually used, the ways in which usage comes to exceed the impositions of formatting, and how the positionality of Black residency identifies the necessity of maximizing the disruptions of such formatting that involve all of "us."

So the frequent invocation of "we" is not to elide this fact but rather to emphasize those dimensions of urban spatiality and practice that demand us to be disrupted, albeit in different directions and orientations. Because as the exact nature of the surrounds—its shapes, timings, and approaches— may indeed differ for different kinds of residents, the surrounds is a reality for all residents, but to different degrees and with different implications. For the surrounds is perhaps a key spatializing of the rescaled, paraphrased question issued by Achille Mbembe in numerous lectures: Who does the city belong to? This is a question answerable only through the inclusion of all its inhabitants. If the city, or as Mbembe explicitly says, the earth, belongs to all its inhabitants, then the critical challenge is how to compose the "we," which must sustain a radical openness to the world through negotiations and compromise. It is a "we," then, that is continuously experimental. So the use of "we" here is as if these thoughts were being delivered on a street corner, in passing, and on the move, and as if in the midst of the surrounds themselves, which would then demand a colloquial usage of "we."

Space, Time, Practice

This book has a simple organization: three chapters and a brief coda focusing on spaces, temporalities, and practice. The first chapter on spaces situates the problematics around capture and liberation within *this* world and not in the becoming of alternative, new worlds. The intent of this emphasis is to focus less on what is to come and rather on what might be here, present, right now, amidst the interregnums, crevices, and no-man's-lands produced by the way in which urbanization stitches and weaves, sutures and distends, a wide array

17

of inclinations, practices, and territories. Articulations never hold for sure, as arrangements fall apart, attention spans waver, and strange complicities ensue in order to buttress collapsing built and social infrastructures. What is it in these moments of disarray that enables momentarily uncontainable seepage, cracks in authority, and attention to spaces that permit different kinds of rehearsals and possibilities from the materials and situations at hand?

The second chapter on temporality is anchored in the proposition of a time when it is possible to forget being forgotten. When the memory of being a victim, of not being fully recognized as one would want or is due, is cast aside in favor of materializing a sense of adequacy without comparison. Here, there is an indifference to the ways in which being abandoned is always marshalled as a threat, and in which any subsequent abandonment is, as Frantz Fanon (2008) holds, a tenuous proposition of invention.

The third chapter is on practice and centers on the position of the *maybe* mentioned earlier, whereby one refutes the prevailing sense of things and the aspiration for guarantees and strategic planning in order to push through a particular "crossing." It is about going where one doesn't belong; showing up without eligibility; taking a chance on everything—all without the prospect of redemption. It is a practice that entails a particular way of seeing, of seeing past the individualized cognitive orientation to see in the surrounds another cognition at work, a constantly mutating array of *calls* emanating from anything and for which there is no clear expectation or right answer. Rather, these calls are invitations to different ways of paying attention, where, again, the surrounds is an accompaniment to everything the resident must do to consolidate a coherent or normative performance, to establish themselves in place. At times, the stakes are enormous, particularly as the costs of failure run higher and higher, as does the capacity for cruelty, particularly on the outskirts of what counts as viable urban life, and yet it is an outskirts to which larger numbers of residents are pushed.

Rebellion without redemption, then, is less railing against the windmills or existential struggles than making commitments to engender something specific. It is the building of an environment replete with propositions not translatable into anything other than themselves; the formation of materials whose compositions and use resist definitive narration. At the same time, the aim of such resistance is less a refusal of integration than carving out a time-limited experiment to configure relations between place, things, and bodies outside of assessment and judgment. Something that takes its place right here and right now, that needs not have anything to do with anything else, that does not seek to defend itself from the outside world but rather seeks to reach it in a different way.

The reflections on rebellion in this chapter are not meant to detract in any way from the long histories of struggle and rebellion by the oppressed. It doesn't steer away from that rebellion's objective of freedom as an invented and valorized way of dealing with the dread of domination and the absolute need to extricate oneself from it (Patterson 2018). It attempts to complement McKittrick's (2021) notions of rebellion without measure, as well as Saidiya Hartman's (n.d., 15) efforts to "exhume open rebellion from the case file," where wayward lives are "liberated from the judgment and classification that subjected young black women to surveillance, arrest, punishment." The chapter seeks to accompany this work with an emphasis on the unanticipated specificities that rebellion can open up as *just* rebellion, sometimes undertaken with a surfeit of irony, indifference, a sense of interminable vulnerability or the insufficiency of any response (Joronen and Rose 2020), or just plain fun.

Amiri Baraka allegedly would remark that the favorite saying of the great Black classical saxophonist Albert Ayler regarding his music was, "It isn't about you," which meant that Ayler was implicitly talking about himself. At the peak of his powers in the late 1960s and early 1970s, Ayler's music was regarded either as an unbearable panoply of squawks, belches, and screams or as the embodiment of revolutionary sensibility, the definitive howl of unrelenting rebellion. Ayler was never that interested in clarifying countervailing interpretations and insisted that musical notation, the system of any inscription prescribing the progression of music, needed to be *accompanied* by sounds that pierced the distinctions between the joyful and wretched. After all, it wasn't about "you" or "him" but about a voice from elsewhere free to say anything "they" want. Despite being haunted by all kinds of demons that shortened his life—in contrast to the pantheon of elders, like Taylor, Roach, Rollins, Shorter, Mitchell, and Allen, who played or are still playing late into their eighties and nineties—Ayler attempted to be his own accompaniment, a companion species from beyond the pale, even though in all this he insisted that what he was doing was just having fun.

ONE

WITHOUT CAPTURE
FROM EXTINCTION
TO ABOLITION

No theory gives you the power to disentangle
something from its particular surroundings,
that is, to go beyond the particular towards
something we would be able to recognize and
grasp in spite of particular appearances.
—Isabelle Stengers, "Introductory Notes on an
Ecology of Practices"

This initial chapter weaves its way across different themes and spaces. It does
so not to build up a consistent and coherent concept of *the surrounds*. Rather
it treats the surrounds as a kind of refrain. Each time it is invoked, it slightly
alters its reference and sense, yet retains traces of past uses, carrying them forward into new examples and sites. The writing here is informed by improvi-
sational music, in that it focuses on eluding "conceptual capture." As perhaps
the most preeminent commentator on improvisation, George Lewis (2007)
posits that this process is the twinning of agency and indeterminacy, a means
of making anything a potential interlocutor and then instantiating a back-
and-forth process of call-and-response and call again. Lewis's experiments
with live algorithms in musical performances attempt to "sound out" the operations of neural networks, machine consciousness, swarm intelligence, and

chaotic dynamics from a position where nothing is programmed for sure, where the "ensemble" requires a continuous process of mutual composition. The performer cannot do anything they want or whatever comes to mind but neither can they fully anticipate that to which they must respond. It is a process that Lewis calls "negotiability," in which improvisatory practices are attentive to the situational dynamics, cultural memories, and discursive constraints from which any performance emerges but at the same time engender what he calls "a mobility of temporalities," a changeableness in the very condition of a performer having to listen and respond.

As such, this book seeks to establish real possibilities for spaces without capture, while also knowing full well that capture, right now, remains omnipresent. So instead of being caught in contradictions, it destabilizes its own ground. The effort leaves tracks, of course, but it also covers them up at the same time; so it may not be always clear how one section of the chapter has necessarily led to another. There is a fair amount of repetition to assist the reader in "keeping track" of what is taking place. But like the itineraries of migrants and city dwellers, which preoccupy my formal research work these days, routes are circuitous, full of detours and impulsive wrong turns, which nevertheless uncover some unanticipated usefulness along the way. One moves not so much to reach a specific destination as to concretize the changeability of what counts as a viable place to stand still, for now.

Not Yet Settled for Sure

Most everyone will remember that as children we were warned about some places that were off-limits, that we were forbidden to enter. The places were referred to as dangerous neighborhoods, the domains of monsters or unseen and unpredictable forces, places that posed an array of physical or moral dangers. We, too, as children might have attributed to particular places a wide range of potential hazards, unbearable uncertainties; these places provoked mixtures of fear and desire, curiosity and repulsion. We might have often just breached the borders of the forbidden, rarely venturing beyond the sight of safety, but intent on testing the waters, trying to contain an oft irrepressible excitement that lives could be so abruptly altered or taken away altogether. In its simplest version, these places, always at a shifting threshold between the actual and imagined, are one way of approaching *the surrounds*. Usually spatialized as something "out" or "over there," just beyond the town or village, just on the other side of the tracks, we know, too, that such surrounds can also be located at the heart of any inhabitation—a room or drawer that was off-limits. We know that these spaces are also gendered and racialized: who can venture where is contingent on the identities you carry with you.

Thus, the surrounds has no specific geography. For our purposes here, the surrounds is not a specific place, but could be; is not separated out from urban systems, but could be; is not something beyond control, but could be; is not a periphery, but could be. It is an ambiguity, an uncertainty with no clear resolution, no promise that eventual clarification will be possible. This is not because the surrounds is by nature a space of uncertainty. Rather because the surrounds does surround, it is in a relationship with what we feel certain about, what we claim to know; and it is from this vantage point that the identification of what populates the surrounds remains elusive. As adults, we often pass through those places of obsessive childhood dread and fascination and wonder what the big deal was. We realize that the forest, neighborhood, cemetery, abandoned building, or industrial zone was not the purveyor of dark forces. We realize, rather, that if there were ghosts and other instruments of harm, they could have been found anywhere. So it is not as if we never inhabit the surrounds, or that the surrounds is fundamentally uninhabitable. Rather, whatever takes place there, whatever is easily recognized, remains unsettled; there are matters of concern, ways of doing things that simply cannot be settled for sure.

What does this have to do then with the consideration "from *extinction* to *abolition*"? We are by now well familiar with the line that crosses these two terms: in a world where an atmosphere of anti-blackness prevails, where certain bodies are arbitrarily expendable and extinguishable simply because they are Black—and for no other reason—the possibility of sustaining human life as a species remains impossible. For in consolidating a specific version of human life that was possible only through denying the terms of that same life to others who purportedly shared such species classification, it becomes impossible to ground the actions necessary to change our orientation to the earth in any discourse of the human. Anti-blackness has long operated as the rehearsal for a truncated, partial, and thoroughly normalized rendition of human life that has institutionalized the acceptance of wasting, of life that can be wasted and made extinct (Gordon 2010, 2013; M. Jackson 2020). If life can be wasted, then so, too, can any other entity that inhabits our world. It is not only that blackness is denigrated, the body taken only as flesh to be rendered a commodity or exotic, but that blackness, in constituting a near-universal surrounds—as something that cannot be settled for sure—is rendered inert, incapable of being anything more than it is, an eternal errancy that warrants continuous capture (Weheliye 2014).

As Ruth Wilson Gilmore (2021) has continuously asserted, abolition is about changing everything; it is a movement toward disproportion, beyond calculations of suitable measures. It is about eliminating all possibilities of capture, any notion of a proper place. There are so many scholars whose work far exceeds my capacity to discuss this relationship between extinction and abolition and whose work shows how abolition is the only means by which to restitute the human capacity to rework a sustainable relationship with the earth, that I will leave the details of abolitionist work to others. Certainly the conceptualizations offered here could not have been made without the work of Katherine McKittrick, Saidiya Hartman, Fred Moten, Tina Campt, Zaire Dinzey-Flores, Jordanna Matlon, Marisol LeBrón, Hortense Spillers, Mariame Kaba, Robin D. G. Kelley, Kelly Gillespie, David Marriott, and Achille Mbembe.

My work here is to think how the surrounds remains a generative, though not necessarily clearly virtuous, domain of blackness, always coming to life in ways not easily or if ever recognized, and how this surrounds operates as an integral aspect of contemporary urbanization. In other words, urbanization continues to be informed by anti-blackness and thus, by implication, is surrounded by a blackness that remains both on the outskirts of normative urban settlement and as an invisible interior. Thus, the restless extensivity of urbanization, its seemingly viral spread across all kinds of landscapes, its folding in of disparate ways of living, connotes not only an insatiable demand for extraction but an accelerating sense of being unsettled (McKittrick 2013; Heynen 2016; Thomas 2016; Alves 2018).

The takings never stop, but how the taken land and resources are actually used, despite all kinds of measures and policing, retains something that cannot be defined for sure. If living as Black requires shifting proportionalities of restraint, indifference, rage, dissimulation, generosity, and overachievement, the sheer heterogeneity of such a repertoire of performance signals spaces beyond capture within the present (Wright 2015; Moten 2017; Ferreira da Silva 2018; Terrefe 2018). I want then to talk about the surrounds as those spaces beyond capture, not immune to it, not free of it, but rather as something aside from it, as loci of continuous rebellion. This is rebellion that might not always look like rebellion. Often bordering on a kind of wretchedness that is nearly impossible to look at directly, that is far from being anywhere near pretty, such rebellion nevertheless enables us to stay focused on seeing something in the now, of making what we have presently available in a different way. The surrounds then are not only those of social refuse and refusal but also those of re-fusing and remaking that *accompany* such refusal. So this work is not about specific political tactics or even political critique, but rather about disorientations, living slightly askew, but ever active in terms of pulling together, putting things together.

This World and Only This World

Several years ago I coauthored a book, *New Urban Worlds*, with my dear friend and long-term comrade Edgar Pieterse. In this book we attempted to categorize the multiplicity of urbanization processes and dispositions, identify the potentialities and arrangements that might already exist within the cities we inhabit, and address the ways in which existent technical affordances, including those of policy and political mobilizations of an urban majority, might enhance the prospects of provisioning, livelihood, and sustainability. While in some respects the title reflects the wishes of the publisher for a catchy title, we acceded to it by virtue of our sensibility that valorizes the capacities of long-occluded Southern urban experiences as a critical epistemology and as a means by which to advocate for a more pluriversal orientation to the practices of inhabitation exemplified by urban majorities in the Southern latitudes.

Perhaps conditioned by the pandemic months of 2020 and 2021, during which one could be everywhere and nowhere all at the same time, I want to partially backtrack on this sense of multiple new worlds—but not because I believe that it is impossible to conceive of new versions of humanity, which the notion of a "world" usually points to, or because I believe that we should hold back on the abolitionist imperative to change everything. Rather, my nascent reticence at operating under the rubric of *new urban worlds* comes from an appreciation of the importance of thinking without narratives of generative relationality, without the conviction that imagines a particular destination, thinking that, through mobilization and determined planned action, works its way toward fruition. This is not because such aspirations and concerted political and technical work are not important. Rather, I want to think through what lurks in the background, what already constitutes the incipient formation of that which we would seem to aspire to and work for.

Instead of new worlds on the horizon, we have perhaps only *this world*, if we have any at all. In its specificity, this world doesn't point to anything else; it is not positioned in a process of incessant becoming. While permutations of things and bodies within this world might be inexhaustible, there is something in the obdurate, sometimes tenacious repetitiveness of patterns and dispositions that frustrates a popular intellectual proposition that there is no world, no set of conditions, that we inevitably belong to (Barber 2016). For that proposition says: if the human simply signals the intertwining of aspiration and the technical affordances that both materialize and motor such aspiration—all the continuous and accelerating updating of the tools that have shaped the possibilities of self-consideration and history—it should be possible to dispense with the very need for a world (Naas 2015; Cohen 2016).

So, why is it *this world* and not a multiplicity of new worlds? Given that we certainly do not have everything we need—since the necessity of aspiration always undoes the sufficiency of whatever is present—can't an expansive recalibration of archives and artistry eventually catapult us into a different orbital landing, where everything has been remade and just? Why is it that we only have just this world? Of course, the specification of "world" is crucial, especially since the "world" does not line up with earth, planet, society, *terroir*, metaphysical object, geography, ecosystem, cosmos, humanity, Gaia, or polity, even though it dips and dabs in all of these to convey itself. For the world is the possibility of narration and analogy; all that exists can be translated into a new image. The weak will become strong, the strong, weak; some fundamental relationality ties together everything that exists in a shifting terrain of mutual implication. As such, the forms of relationships that exist now are always being reworked by others, giving us the sense that we are on our way, on our way somewhere where the separations of terms, of you and me, us and them, Black and white, are finally reconciled in an equilibration of sense and possibility (Colebrook 2012, 2014).

But when Gilles Deleuze (1997) indicates that we only have *this world*, what he seems to be saying is that there are relationships that cannot be analogized, that this world embodies forces so intense and opaque that whatever technical affordances, aspirations, or will we might possess is simply insufficient to retain a relationship with this world that enables a sense of forward action. All these are insufficient to generate a story that sustains the mutually enlivening intersection of the world's components, whether nature, cities, or cultures. While that which is broken might seem to be the very basis for a hoped-for resolution in a new world, Deleuze sees this brokenness, of being without a world, without the possibilities of a progressive, sustained relationship among things, as mediated by thought and desire, as the prerequisite for being in the world.

Being is something necessarily broken and, as such, subject to repair; and repair itself is the lineage and methodology of relationships (S. Jackson 2019). Repair keeps things going, but the repaired is not the same as it was before, for the repair doesn't cure, it does not transform or transfix (S. Jackson 2014). Repair often borrows parts from elsewhere; it often bypasses problems rather than dealing with them directly. Repair may exacerbate certain underlying conditions in attempts to address the symptoms of disfunction. Once something is broken, it never fully returns to being itself (Graham and Thrift 2007; Crosby and Stein 2020). One often hears that "the system is beyond repair," that the society is so broken that only revolutionary change will set things right. And certainly many instances of brokenness cannot be repaired.

Repair is not a panacea for all that goes wrong; and repair often intrudes on the scene replete with either an excess of good intentions and little skill or an excess of skill with little long-term imagination. Yet, by having only *this world*, what we have is an arena in which each in its brokenness and insufficiency requires the immediacy of a response or engagement that necessitates a decision, an assessment, and often an improvised intervention utilizing whatever is on hand (McLaren 2018). Although there are certainly "planned repairs," as indicated in the signage one sees across many cities, brokenness implies in each instance a sense of temporariness, of the transitory. Brokenness, while in some instances truly signaling the end of things, is also something that need not be inevitable. While one might have to wait for repairs or tolerate incremental, stopgap measures until more comprehensive repairs might be made, what is affirmed is the transitory nature of our relationships within the ambit of this world, a sense of tentativeness and fragility that accompanies any endeavor (Cesafsky 2017).

We are never at home in this world, not because this world does not provide a home (Derrida 2000; M. Jackson 2000). Certainly we are wrapped up in discursive and material operations that enable us to anchor ourselves in place, to have a perspective or worldview. We certainly are offered the stability of a set of relations that will see us through a developmental process from childhood to old age. It is not because wherever we find ourselves is already broken, even as this is probably the case. Rather, we are never at home in this world because home itself is a repair of something that always takes place somewhere else. Home is not primarily a place of refuge or socialization or care but a mobile instrument always being inserted elsewhere to repair the brokenness of offices, factories, schools, and so forth. Home is that sense that at the end of the day, the primacy of experiencing home as the nonsubstitutable anchorage of one's relationship to the world will make up for the uncertainties and disparities that characterize relationships elsewhere, will ward off brokenness, even as homes themselves are broken all the time (Mitropoulos 2012, 2019; Cooper 2017).

27

We have only this world, however broken our relationship to it might be, and Deleuze expresses faithfulness to this relationship because it is something always in need of repair; as such, we are not captured by this relationship, even if it may be the only one that we have. In this temporality of transitory functioning, of no guarantees about eventual outcomes, what matters is *this* time, *this* instance, what can be done with the tools we have now. What relations can be configured to access materials and capacities to act expeditiously, to minimize the suffering entailed, and reduce the prospects for long-term damage?

This does not mean that a fundamental capacity to aspire is attenuated, in part, because the nature of such aspiration is not ours alone. It is embedded within the very technicities that we rely on in order to act and reflect on action. Every instance of a technical system, whether simple tools or complex computation machineries, suggests its own prospective courses of action, materializes not only the operations of its current assemblages but posits in its very design and functioning the basis of unanticipated courses of action and its concomitant social arrangements (Hui 2015, 2018). Certainly the insurrectional moments that characterized the year 2020 could not have taken hold or been so widespread without the proliferation of citations, images, and synchronous collective actions conveyed through social medias, which functioned to generate imaginaries and new scaled possibilities of social change.

Territories of Operation

What I want to emphasize here are the ways in which relations to this world are predicated not only on a preexistent brokenness of coherence and coordination but on the ways in which such brokenness, fragmentation, and dispersal usher in practices of repair or invention that provisionally suture together bits and pieces of places into territories of operation. This is particularly the case for those volitionally or involuntarily unsettled within the urban regions of Asia and Africa that I have worked in throughout my career. Here, territories of operation simply refer to channels, conduits, passageways, and openings through which life can be enacted in ways beyond capture in oppressive carceral situations—whether actual prisons, households, or neighborhoods (Escobar 2008; Raffestin 2012; Clare, Habermehl, and Mason-Deese 2018).

Deprived of any essential analogic system that provides an overarching measure of coherence to the city or region, territories of operation become the outcomes of particular itineraries of repair. Etching out their own circuits

1.1 | Material resistance. Photograph by Michele Lancione.

across infrastructures that are often unfinished, detached, ruined, or adamantly still public, increasing numbers of urban residents use the mobility of their bodies, their tactics of spatial immersion, their social contacts, provisional occupations, and feigned uselessness to connect discrepant spaces of the city to each other—sites of temporary dwelling, domains of exchange and reciprocal care (Simone 2014; Furniss 2016; Caldeira 2012). Just as important as repair might be to the viability of everyday life, there are also times when it is important to leave what seems broken alone, untouched. For brokenness potentially offers new premises for action: trees that emerge from broken sidewalks, or the nocturnal solitude offered by a wrecked car on the side of the road. While brokenness is an incitement to repair, a reiteration of the viability of *this world*, brokenness can also suggest its own courses of action without our being lured into doing something about it (Kemmer 2019).

This process of making territories of operation is, in many respects, completely logistical in that it is configured to facilitate the movement of things with minimal impediment—even if the thing is simply the body of the resident (Neilson 2012; Martin 2012; Rossiter 2014). While these territories of operation may not be readily consolidated or stabilized, as the fundamental relations of inhabitation and questions of citizenship and racialization remain broken, they nonetheless constitute a locus of efficacy and self-valorization that places many residents, who previously had no platform of touch, in touch

29

with each other . What an accruing archive of itineraries in aggregate actually does in terms of effectively altering the structures of power within urban life is difficult to measure. Certainly the need for more visible and, if you will, standardized formats of political mobilization is not obviated.

But whether these mobilizations are themselves possible may be contingent on new vectors of movement and interchange that temporarily exceed the fantasies of different regimes to fix the city once and for all. It goes beyond the image of absolute logistical efficiency where everything is in its place through a system of calculation, transport, and tracking capable of taking everything out of its place. What is particularly salient to this discussion is the degree to which many residents are on the move, living through these improvised itineraries. They certainly cannot go anywhere they want. They certainly are restricted to spaces that are alternately depleted, underdeveloped, failed, or replete with generic or racialized built environments. But at the same time, this movement is a deferral of resolution. Residents might still profess a desire for "our house, with two cats in the yard," but they are in actuality wary of settling anywhere too prematurely, even if they have the means to do so.

In many cities of the Global South, the continuously reworked contours of the metropolitan state assume new intricacies across what Neferti Tadiar (2022) has called the cash rewards/kickbacks/rents/protection money/promotion logics of police–political machines. Although the methods vary from one urban region to another, from the use of religious dogma to drug eradication to terrorist control, the very intimacies of social life are targeted in such a way as to foster increasing levels of distrust among neighbors and to promote the adoption of defensive maneuvers by individuals in an attempt to exert control over how a household or an individual is to be known. A concordance of policing strategies, the profusion of media messages about individual success and responsibility, the voluminous demands on neighborhood life and infrastructures that increase the labor intensity of everyday management, and the general undermining of platforms for public deliberation contribute to an intensifying individualizing of the practices of urban residency (Zeiderman 2016; Abourahme 2018; Warburg and Jensen 2018).

In addition, this is accompanied by an amplified sense of *mattering,* where a more proficient and detailed assessment of the behavior of residents, their practices and aspirations, comes to matter for how they are to be governed and enrolled in various trajectories of development. Determinations about eligibility—in terms of access to benefits, rights, spaces of operation and residence, provisioning, and investment—become increasingly critical. No matter the background, residents increasingly matter in terms of what might be extracted from them, even if it simply entails the probability of them acting in particular ways within a wide range of different scenarios (Beller 2018; Benjamin 2019; Sadowski 2020). This reduction of the horizon of how human life will count forecloses other imaginations of *mattering* that expand the range of relationalities persons might have, and do have, with various materiality (Coole and Frost 2010; Manning and Massumi 2014; Savransky 2016).

At the same time, the individual decisions, dilemmas, and actions of individuals and households increasingly matter for residents themselves, as the implications of failure and wrong moves might have dire and irreversible consequences. This is particularly the case for households that are able to consume more by being offered more opportunities to take on debt. The reluctance then of "circulating residents" to settle down, to apply limited resources toward consolidating a new place for themselves, even as they are often being forcibly resettled, not only reflects a hedging on a broad toolbox of possible actions in a context where they report difficulties in assessing where the city is going and what will be required of them (Amin 2016). It also reflects an approach to urban life that concedes its brokenness: broken in terms of any overarching sense of connection among its different sectors and places; broken in terms of what individuals might have aspired to in terms of an incremental progression toward the "good life"; and broken in terms of the willingness and capacity of those who govern to provide either a persuasive imaginary of a well-functioning city or the technical and political competence to deliver the basics of urban provisioning. In conceding the brokenness, the incentive to repair not only draws on long-honed practices of ensuring the infrastructural and social endurance of specific neighborhoods. It also elaborates repair as everyday practices of individuals reconnecting their relationships with the urban world, a world that is not conceived as new or necessarily multiple, but the only world that they have (Knox 2017).

Repair, again, concerns the quilting of the fragments, the lines residents draw among different hostels, boarding rooms, sweatshops, junkyards, vacated warehouses, underpopulated industrial zones, vast swathes of affordable single-family housing, and massive apartment blocks. While bodies are indeed moved around, it would be a mistake to say that large numbers of residents are being expelled from the city. For the city stretches along uncertain trajectories and hybrid recompositions that, although distant from the cores, distant from the high-value–generating zones of accumulation, nevertheless constitute a staging area for actions that are, at the moment, nebulous in part because the terrain is itself nebulous (Addie and Keil 2015; Jensen 2015, 2017; Gordillo 2019).

31

I want to think through these spaces of simultaneous fugitivity, displacement, targeted extraction, and recomposition as the *urban surrounds*. These surrounds are not necessarily emplaced in the peripheries or hinterlands of urban regions, even though these sites perhaps provide the most opportune site from which to think about and engage them. The surrounds also include zones within the urban core that implicitly or intentionally refuse incorporation into the predominant logics of accumulation or circuits of extraction. Still, their physical proximity to the centers of accumulation, urban renewal, and speculation mean that they are often deeply recessed into the interstices separating different infrastructures; in between parking garages, ports, railheads; in the backlots and vague spaces between megatowers. The surrounds have no essential integrity of form or functioning.

At times, they are spaces in waiting, spaces of storage, of the warehousing of devalued populations. At times, they are the spaces where the curve of ascendancy has been flattened for a prolonged period; where residents are stuck with nonfungible assets, or in locations repeatedly vulnerable to flooding or conflict. The surrounds can even encompass those anachronistic domains of power and administration that no longer function according to their constitutional principle—where authority, privilege, and money have moved on, leaving vacuous bureaucracies in their wake that become either living mausoleums or the vectors of a multiplicity of arrangements in which documents, approvals, stamps, permissions, and licenses are issued for a cut of the action (Blundo 2006; Gupta 2012; Hull 2012). The surrounds is by definition unruly, unsettled, provisional, unspecified.

There are two particular notions I have in mind with this sense of the surrounds. First, that the surrounds is a liminal interstice in between multiple, diverging trajectories of urbanization that are always in the process of being sutured, more or less. Second, that the surrounds is a fundamental *accompaniment in movement* to any specific force or factor in urbanization, regardless of its logic or history, and exists as something that *could be*, an undefined supplement that fuses moments of doubt, unease, or irritability in the coherence of any such force, but whose operations and shape largely remain independent of it. This is more a matter of how things move toward and away from each other, itineraries of circulation rather than disruptive supplements to things seemingly fixed in place.

These ideas about the surrounds are not intended to displace the critical observations that have been made by those working on processes of extended

1.2 | A capacious surrounds. Photograph by Michele Lancione.

urbanization in the years since this notion was issued by Henri Lefebvre (2014). Particularly important is Lefebvre's sense of how urbanization extends itself beyond the operations and arrangements that initially consolidated its specific forms, where urbanization became its own driving impetus not as a cohered set of economic and political processes but rather as an axiomatic capable of generating a plethora of novel dispositions, even if their viability entailed the production of surplus value. Here the work of Christian Schmid (2015, 2018), Neil Brenner (2015, 2019), Roger Keil (2018), and Roberto Monte Mor (2018) has been particularly valuable. But having invoked these more strictly geographical interventions, I want to refer to notions that concur with the sense of the surrounds as "not this, but could be," where its nature is not captured in any specific manifestation but can nevertheless manifest itself in forms and situations that do not inherently belong to it.

The work of Frédéric Neyrat might provide some useful scaffolding to this notion of the surrounds. In his critique of so-called geo-constructivism, Neyrat (2018) warns about orientations that continuously affirm infinite and immanent generativity. By this he means the endless capacity for becoming

33

that informs the conceit of actors who believe that the earth can be terra-formed, made available to numerous ameliorative interventions that will ensure the sustainability of the earth as a viable place for humans.

But humans are now aggregated as a univocal species, whose prior differentiation can no longer be afforded in the need to recalibrate new relationships with nature, which has largely been a phantasmic construction of humans. In both the conceptualization of nature as something intrinsically removed from society or as something intrinsically a part of and an enfolding of everything, nature is available to be acted on, for better or worse. For Neyrat, nature is neither a figment of our imagination nor an all-encompassing unity but rather what he calls a *traject*, a long-term event of unfolding differentiation, concretized in different forms at different times.

What is important here is that becoming itself is contingent on separation, constraint, and withdrawal: something that is recessed from view, not apparent or traceable; that which permits rhythm, a declension, a gap, a pause, an empty space in syncopated time. Not dissimilarly, if the urban is the site of endless productivity, a compulsion to remake, refine, recalibrate, then it can never really emplace, put down roots or anchor. Rather, processes of urbanization generate all kinds of untoward implications. These implications don't move toward anything in particular; they don't necessarily produce something clearly functional, useful, or continuous. This is evident in the sudden shifts in direction that often occur in the development of new urban spaces across the near-hinterlands of many urban regions, where new built environments "come and go," sometimes attaining clear functionality and at other times providing no clear sense of where they are heading. Neyrat calls this "the unconstructable"—a universal reserve of disconnection, without which differences could not exist. These are gaps in the narratives that articulate and refigure various manifestations of the urban into specific relationships.

Production is not only generative but dissipative, as the entwining of colonial and climate histories clearly demonstrates. And production increasingly obscures the elements and processes of making, so that it is not apparent what actually exists or how to relate to it. As such, antiproduction maneuvers are required to interrogate how particular things appear, how they got where they are and acquired the status they did. This is a maneuver that goes beyond the simple affirmation of identifying the positionalities of something within an endless meshwork of relationships that would demonstrate the ways in which everything is available to each other. Rather, antiproduction entails the ways in which human and inhuman inhabitants compose an environment that *renders* each accessible to the other, laying out together the *manner* in which human and inhuman inhabitants and the environment come to exist with each other. Otherwise, if I simply say that I am inextricably linked to you, then acting on you is as if I am acting on me, something to which I am entitled by the exigency of my survival. You thus become accessible to me without a mutual deliberation on the terms of that access, something that reiterates the basic tropes of the colonial and undermines or at least limits your access to this world. Antiproduction is also a maneuver that speculatively considers the circumstances under which someone or something out there would have nothing to do with me. What would it take for relationships not to occur? What are the cuts, fragmentations, and divides that are inserted to curtail relations? Under what circumstances and with what strategic tools are these separations at least momentarily overcome? How might such cuts be retained strategically for a particular period of time? What and where are all of the ties that continue to bind even when relations seem broken? How does brokenness itself suggest the endurance of relations that appear, empirically, not to be present at all?

For difference to mean something concretely, in terms of an economy of affordances and mutual action, might require a process of what Brigitta Kuster (2017) calls *becoming everyone*. This is a process of becoming no one in particular, a generic disidentification, where plentitude is held in compressed form, where any set formula of eligibility or value is unable to determine how the entities gathered are aligned with each other or the proportions of their relative contributions to the operations of the whole.

For if our access to each other can repeat the colonial situation of extraction and theft, there must be spaces of inaccessibility. When the surrounds are now for the most part temporarily concretized in certain environments at the urban hinterlands, it is exactly accessibility that is being unconstructed. This also was the case for certain core urban areas, such as New York's Lower East Side at the advent of the twentieth century or Harlem during the 1920s, or Tower Hamlets (London) for much of its contentious history. Most recently, the East London Mosque, a powerful institution coordinating not only a large congregation and substantial reserves but an extensive network of health, education, housing, and social services, exerted almost total control over Tower Hamlet's local government from 2010 to 2015. This was a means of reiterating the antiracist struggles of the 1980s and altering the accessibility of the borough's built and social environments to penetration from global capital working outwards from London City's financial center. This political move attempted to constitute an alternative trajectory of accumulation, using many of the same speculative tools on land and real estate but purportedly in the interest of the borough's working-class majority. It was an attempt to reroute the decision-making apparatus through a multiplicity of hybridized organizations through which the Mosque both extended itself and also availed to a wide range of grassroots quasi organizations to concretize and extend their local interests—all in a manner of structural opacity. It wasn't so much that the predominant Muslim actors were intent on operating through networks of secrecy, but rather that the dispersed institutional forms intersecting with the official apparatuses of the local state were not readily legible in terms of the commonly accepted vernaculars of administration.

In the mushrooming Jakarta landscapes of warehouses, cheap single-family forty-square-meter pavilions, mega–apartment complexes, upscale gated communities, industrial parks, migrant hostels, and shophouse-styled commercial zones it is clear that a vast urban expansion is taking place, a blanketing of different modes of settlement. At the same time, an equally vast vacancy endures as these projects are never ever fully completed or—if they are—not yet fully used or occupied. It doesn't mean that at some point they won't be, or that they can't be repurposed or torn down for other projects. It just means that, at the moment, they remain unavailable for any accounting for sure, any definitive judgment of their efficacy. Additionally, this enduring emptiness for now also troubles the conditions of those who do occupy and remain. It raises questions about their own aspirations and agendas and their own perceptions of the meanings of the spaces they navigate and what is workable and permissible or not, often cultivating highly idiosyncratic responses.

For example, in some local town councils, unofficial rules are tightened and local surveillance measures are intensified. Yet in others they are simply let go as residents become indifferent to everyday comportment, household compositions, and activities. Sometimes these contrasting orientations leave each alone; at other times and in other circumstances, new accommodations and differences emerge that allow for new uses to be made of underutilized commercial, residential, or industrial spaces in a series of trade-offs or bartering (Cornea, Véron, and Zimmer 2017; Kundu and Chatterjee 2020). Here goods and services are revalued in terms of their support for experimental ventures, providing new objects of governance for local administrations concerned that they are being hemmed in by context-insensitive protocols. So the surrounds are not one thing, neither always transparent nor opaque, neither always generative nor withholding. They are at times the grounds for a more thorough and judicious accounting of the manner in which beings and things are available to each other, and at other times the grounds for the impossibility of any kind of assessment. They are the trajectory of the urban, not as a self-replicating fractalized machine that simply repeats the same formula as a means of extending space and extending itself across it. Rather, the urban is also that which breaks open, pauses, and compresses. All these maneuvers are unproductive in any strict sense but worthy in terms of what Michael Fischer (2018) calls the temporality of "in the meantime."

Tools of the "In the Meantime"

To elaborate on this "meantime," I draw on the project of J. Kameron Carter and Sarah Jane Cervenak, who, following Saidiya Hartman's (1997) injunction to always imagine an outside while being inside, to make one's way into a "black outdoors," assembled a group of leading Black studies scholars in 2016–17 at Duke University to consider the ways in which Black living points to the possibilities of a space within this world beyond enclosure, property, and self-possession. What are the legacies and potentials of Black study that enable the specification of practices operating outside sovereignty, specification, measurement, and capitalist valuation and that can be experienced within the enclosures of racial capital?

The conundrum here is that these outdoors are only graspable as broken, since the discernible and conclusive rendering of the outside as the normative inside is yet to come. As broken, they are necessarily partial but reparable. But they are reparable only in terms of not restoring them to health—as such a practice is inevitably informed by the "cures" issued by an inside. Nevertheless, such repair is directed toward maintaining the endurance of an outdoors, recognizing both that the brokenness cannot be fixed within the master's domain or within his terms and how such brokenness is the very means of reestablishing a relationship with this world from an outside, from a relationship to it that is broken.

This is not a place of a fundamental negativity, antagonism, or contradiction but a position that enables one to regard this world as already an outdoors. This position does not affirm brokenness as the inevitable enduring condition of this world. Rather, it is the starting point of a reorientation able to resist any settlement on offer, any formula of reconciliation, any proposition that offers a way out or a renewed relationship that does not prioritize the active appropriation of the broken as the very material from which to constitute a form of totality. Because such a totality remains situated within the racialized apparatuses of spatial control, it must configure its own strange visibilities recognized as neither "this" nor "that."

Here, I also want to invoke the Islamic notion of *bilad al-siba,* a space that is not addressable in any available vernacular, a space of disorder and illegitimacy, unsettled and disconnected, and, finally, a practice of living at the enemy's expense (Brachet and Scheele 2019). These multiple connotations do not suggest a space prohibitive of inhabitation or use but rather the need for transience, momentary renditions of what is made available pulled into the image of a settled territory that at the same time remains unruly. As unruly, this space is not so much interested in perpetuating itself as interested in acting as a platform for "moving on," repositioning everyone entailed in these arrangements into new neighborhoods of affiliation and collective action.

Questions of rendering have long been at the heart of so-called peripheral worlds, the constantly shifting assemblages of "we" among people with a tentative anchorage in the familiar tropes of kinship, ethnicity, and territory. Here, the "affinal" is based not on reciprocal exchange or common belonging but on raiding, stealth, exorbitant displays, transgressive expenditure, simulation, "strange" alliances, and transmutations with spirits, ghosts, and djinn (Brachet and Scheele 2016; Brachet 2018; Scheele 2018). If all broken relationships require some kind of mediation, some kind of brokerage and bargains, then for peripheral Muslim worlds, djinn have long been critical intermediaries, breaking and repairing and breaking again, so that dispensations are not settled for sure, so that hierarchies are dissolved only to be refigured again and broken (Alidou 2005). For djinn are the interlocutors, or the hinges of territories that intersect spirit bargains, money transfers, remembrances of saints, reequipped 4×4s, collective traumas, navigational circuits, and practices of hospitality.

Today, the Sahel-Saharan regions long associated with *bilad al-siba* struggle to piece together viable territories of operation that are capable of compensating for the paucity of state investments. This is due in part to the residues of colonial attributions that saw Sahelian populations as those without control, limited statehood, and replete with conflicts between herding and farming on shrinking volumes of arable land (Turner et al., 2011; Ribot, Faye, and Turner 2020). This region's population is intensely heterogeneous, more or less Muslim, more or less anchored in discernible national identities, more or less Black, and so forth. Within an expanding regime of surveillance; plentiful guns; thousands of religious institutions and sentiments; oscillating flows of narcotics, cigarettes, and pharmaceuticals; shifting porosities across national borders; internecine conflicts among ethnic groups expressing divergent means for realizing common aspirations; and interventions of foreign forces, constellations of actors attempt to instantiate themselves across often highly differentiated communities (Hüsken and Klute 2015). They do this as a way of providing protection, securing a base for trafficking, curating interdependencies among diverse local authorities, and aligning themselves with widely known antagonists, such as an array of Jihadi groupings, in order institute new mechanisms of accumulation and distribution (Bencherif, Campana, and Stokemerl 2020).

Widely misrepresented as conflicts among different global Islamic mafias, such as the Islamic State or al-Qaeda, these constellations, more or less associated with specific ethnic groups, not only attempt to enhance their capacities for circulation but themselves circulate among different organizational formats and alliances, whichever is best suited in giving voice to a panoply of opportunities to become local service providers (Retaillé and Walther 2012; Raineri and Strazzari 2015). There is a recognition here that all opportunities are transitory. Thus, while the profits accruing largely to Tilemsi Arabs in Northern Mali through the trans-shipment of cocaine from Guinea and Guinea Bissau to Algeria and Libya were enormous, there was also always a sense that it wouldn't last. For the technical apparatuses needed for this economy—vehicles, routes, drivers, protection, weapons, payoffs, laundering—always suggested alternate assemblages that they would not be able to control (Julien 2011; Ojo 2020). So they always hedged their investments across different products, affiliations, and identifications. What was important was to render the appearance of a well-ordered machine for the time being. While insufficient, in and of itself, for a prolonged duration, it could provide adequate cover in the medium term to test the waters in other domains, as well as prop up other economies such as herding, with which a particular group was long associated, even if only for symbolic reasons.

With the notions of the Black outdoors and *bilad al-siba*, I suggest the surrounds not only as an ever-shifting domain of possibility that exists simply by looking at the urban in a different way, although that process can be useful, but rather as one that exists through an enactment of circulation, repeated and recalibrated as itineraries. These itineraries render specific spaces, apprehended as fundamentally broken, into the materials for provisional sutures used to constitute territories of operation in the interstices between ever-shifting technologies of spatial control and the capacity of the settled to *undo*, as Hartman (n.d.) puts it, the very parameters of recognition that otherwise divide the worthy and unworthy, the obedient and the wayward, the lost and the found. The surrounds are what residents *do* rather than a reference to something that is there. Although what is there is rendered useful, to a point.

39

Oscillating Urbanscapes

Consider the ways in which the models of urban development tend to err in favor of upward projections, the ability of each new building to handle potential demand, to avoid price inflation based on scarcity, and to manage possible multiplier effects that are envisioned as the outcome of the intensified urbanization of spaces. Part of the ability of developers to raise the necessary finances for their projects is to represent them as bigger and better than they have a reasonable chance of becoming. In financing schemes that must cover debt accrued for past project development, the terms of new projects have to be inflated accordingly, so that new projects are sometimes conceived as an instrument to more firmly consolidate the asset class of those past (Halbert and Rouanet 2014; Halbert and Attuyer 2016).

As a result, and at different scales, urban landscapes are increasingly carpeted with underutilized projects and built environments that often become the way stations of many different kinds of temporary use. As populations are pushed out farther away from places of employment, many residents holding on in more proximate locations convert a portion of the spaces they can access into temporary, cheap rental accommodations—so that others might save on transportation costs. Households are sometimes distributed across multiple temporary locations in order to cover a wider terrain of potential opportunity, and groups of otherwise tenuously connected persons forge roving bands of "extended families" that move in concert, but not physically together, across both agreed upon and improvised circuits encompassing a wide range of satellite towns where things in general may be much less regulated. Here, conventional modes of settlement are undone, while the attentional spans of related individuals are extended across variegated terrain.

Let me offer a small example: Rachman is part of a *kommunitas* in Jonggol, in the eastern hinterlands of Jakarta, a large expanse of residential, commercial, and industrial zones that has somehow never completely shed its rural feel and whose subsequent spaciousness is deceptive in terms of demographic density and economic operation. The *kommunitas*, to use a popular Indonesian term, simply refers to any form of self-organized collectivity, which in most instances remains largely informal, like an extended network of friends or associates who view themselves as tied together in some kind of common purpose. Here, it is a crew of thirtysomethings, some forty individuals, who have in common only that they attended elementary school in the Javanese city of Sukubumi at the same time. Some of them found work in a food processing plant in Jonggol, working drug-fueled fourteen-hour

40

1.3 | Interstices. Photograph by Michele Lancione.

shifts and sharing single rooms in migrant hostels. When jobs could not be found in the factory, some took up positions as food sellers near the factory gates or drove motorcycle taxis that ferried workers in their attempts to find less oppressive employment elsewhere. Some took jobs as domestics in the households of factory managers, and still others took jobs at small repair shops or cell phone outlets.

Through WhatsApp they checked in with each other throughout the day, conveying information about where to find cheap goods, how to make money on the side, where to find the best affordable healthcare, where local political or religious meetings were being held that offered free food packages, and opportunities for the group to perform collective dissimulations about being some gang, some constituency. Over the years, their residencies, employment, and activities have spread out across an ever-expanding Jonggol. They have become low-level suppliers for surplus goods needed in construction projects, caterers for weddings, promoters of hip-hop events, and brokers for local politicians, and in doing so they have attempted to redraw lines of oscillating connections among a wide range of activities and locations.

One of their crew, Andi, drives a small bus they purchased to ferry their growing number of offspring to a small school they have established in a vacated office block. Everything they have done over the years has been treated as accompaniment to one another. Each person was themselves viewed as an accompaniment to lives that were still led largely on an individual basis but that availed their own surrounds, availed constant challenges to rethink what might go together, how different places and activities might touch on the other, without tying each other down.

To Be Pan-African

This refusal to be tied down has long been the ethos of traders from the Futa Jallon region in Guinea. "We will only discover each other a long way from here," is a common refrain among neighbors. "At home we are surrounded by our enemies, over there, beyond what we know, we make everyone our friends," is another. As my longtime friend and collaborator Amadou Diallo remarked a few days before Guinean president Sékou Touré's death in 1984, African cities are hinges, their primary purpose to set different angles of openings and closure. As hinges, they have no intrinsic identity themselves but are instead modulations of light and darkness. They focus on the alternating perspectives on things, at times widening exposures to some great outdoors, at other times narrowing the gaze, withdrawing observers inward. Diallo started his career at age ten, selling loose cigarettes in the Chicago neighborhood of Conakry. Once a bastion of loyalty to the Pan-African dreams of Touré, the district nonetheless bore the brunt of his paranoia, fed by psychotic mystics from Labé. It was from this mountain town that Diallo had moved to the Guinean capital when he was two years old; these same mountains supplied factory workers for Nanterre, taxi drivers for the Bronx, bankers for Dakar, and gem dealers for Brazzaville.

According to Diallo, hinges were the essential technical feature of thresholds that had to be marked among multiple belongings and realities. They permitted differentiated degrees of access, in turn mediating everyday decisions as to what and where one should be. "Africa is not something you bring home or take with you; not something to believe in or to recognize as you move around," he was fond of saying. "It is only a door never completely open or closed." By this he meant that Africa was literally an "outlook," a shifting vantage point from and through which to engage the world; something that could be narrowed down to a microscopic visibility or widened to take in everything without discrimination or discretion.

As such, the Pan-African dreams that were the stuff of daily tutelage through Diallo's primary and secondary education were not those of some united polity eviscerating colonial borders or those of some consolidation of

Black peoples dispersed across seas. They were something much simpler yet elusive: dreams of spreading out, of being more or less this or that, of offering different versions of oneself to audiences that would never be the same twice. The dreams were those of a life beyond capture, for even as many African societies had been based on the prospect of seizing or being seized, of being captivated by different streams of thought, the ethos of the Futa was essentially "never give anything away." You can be dispossessed, charitable, or sacrifice anything but never show all your cards. Younger and thoroughly urbanized Fulbe from the region would often complain that their elders never told them anything, never shared the essential secrets or wisdom, always invoking that what they needed to know was "right in front of them," if only they could see it, if only they altered the angle by which they looked at things.

Here again, the hinge points to questions of access, touching on the preoccupations of many African societies with the politics of exposure, of modulating just how much of the world can be let in at any given time and what has to remain closed off. In West African Islam, every person is inscribed in and by a specific project that can be realized only through warding off constant attempts by others to extract from it, to dilute or distort it. Thus, what one performs, in all the different versions of oneself that can be dissimulated, on the basis of everything that the project is not, is a constantly moving hinge that never stabilizes the lines of sight and exposure. The life project thus functions as a surrounds. It envelopes the person's life with purpose, yet is constantly elusive to external scrutiny and, thus, judgment. It reserves the right of judgment to no one but Allah, while marking a path where no one is expendable, for each project demands its witnesses, an egalitarian assembly where no one is in a position more privileged than anyone else, since no one knows your project any better than anyone else.

For Amadou Diallo, his project "was always going to be only temporary": the simple mud brick house he acquired from a cousin who was executed by Sékou Touré; his multifarious residencies in some twenty cities across the world and the durations of his stay. His life was always going to be on the move, in order to exist, even as many aspects were replete with permanence. As a young man he bought cloth in Togo and brought it to a simple stall in a peripheral market in Conakry. Decades later he was arranging containers of textiles, electronics, foodstuffs, and hardware from Shenzhen to ports across West Africa. Having spent years shuttling between Bangkok, Dubai, Abidjan, and Conakry, he was one of the first generation of African traders to base themselves in Guangzhou, later spreading out across other Chinese entrepôt before heading to Mumbai when China got "overcrowded."

At first he collected money from family members in the Futa in order to purchase wax cloth from markets in Lomé, to and from which he traveled by road in a string of shared taxis, their roofs piled high with assortments of tarpaulin-covered goods. After the extractions by different versions of police at seemingly endless roadblocks along the route, he made little profit from his arduous efforts and sometimes shifted his forays into more obscure frontier and improvised markets, whose temporary existence sometimes meant that they had already gone by the time he arrived. At the outset, his generosity was a skill, as he went out of his way to display kindness and share information with fellow compatriots, offering to tend to a host of small difficulties that Guineans living or traveling across West Africa had back home. But he rarely said anything about what this help consisted of or much about himself, the helper. What I know is that coming from a family of well-known *marabouts*, Quranic teachers and counsellors, there were networks of contacts in Conakry, Kankan, and Kissidougou—the main trading towns—to which he could appeal and from which he could take orders for different goods. He ingrained himself into the resident Guinean community in Treichville, Abidjan, but then set himself somewhat apart in nearby Koumassi, where he could maneuver more freely outside the rigid Fulbe hierarchies of his home region and make contacts with related Fulani merchants coming from Nigeria, Senegal, and Niger who were also seeking temporary respite from prolonged periods of apprenticeships and obligations to a host of "big men." Operating outside of the order of things, these interchanges and sometimes alliances were maintained under the radar and were largely only temporary. They nevertheless proved useful as a means to establish backdoor channels into otherwise tightly controlled marketing systems.

By the early 1980s word was spreading that Dubai was a cheap place to buy textiles and clothing as well as other consumables. The city had amassed substantial warehouse space, had completed a new port, and was a relatively easy point of access to goods coming from all over Africa. Import fees were low, storage space was cheap, there were almost no controls over exports, and visas were freely available. Initially the acquisition of visas was tied to hotel stays and to brokerage through specific trade- and clearinghouses. While these linkages greatly facilitated efficiencies in emerging trading networks, they were also instituted by the Emirates to ensure temporary stays. But as traders converged on Dubai from across Africa and Asia, the resultant heterogeneity of visitors and activities largely mitigated these controls, and Amadou set up his first trading company, expanding the scope of his purchases to supply markets at the peripheries of Abidjan, Accra, and Conakry to avoid the layers of middlemen that operated as gatekeepers to the major central urban markets. Initially Amadou brought and filled empty suitcases during his early forays to Dubai, but he soon started shifting increased volumes to Porto Novo, Benin, which for years acted as a free port for West Africa.

Islamic connections initially proved important as a means of securing places to stay and store goods outside the official logistical systems. For at every level, Dubai was about repeating temporariness, providing an infrastructure for coming and going without the institutionalization of residence or commerce. Of course, this has substantially changed over the past decades, and Amadou retains several restaurants, a freight forwarding company, and two warehouses in the Deira district. Still, a major move Amadou made was to enroll in an Islamic studies course at the then recently opened University of Sharjah, which subsequently enabled him to deepen and extend his relationships with younger Emiratis who themselves were looking for ways to take advantage of the burgeoning international trade. Amadou then used his trademark generosity to assist other Guinean traders passing through, cultivating their loyalty and work in Guinea as well as in Côte d'Ivoire. This assistance was extended not only to Guinean nationals but also to Africans coming from other regions, and Amadou's ability to purchase property in both Dubai and Sharjah enabled him to establish hospitality centers that could assist with a variety of problems such as documentation, fake brokerage, and onerous fees and custom duties at various African ports of entry.

But in this business, as Amadou puts it, everything "lasts only for the moment." No matter how effectively a trader institutionalizes themselves in a given location or set of trading networks, no matter how much trust is cultivated, the composition of the game and its players exudes volatility and is difficult to stabilize, particularly in the face of a swarm of younger itinerants willing to take cutthroat risks and aiming for quick money. Modulating the necessary balances between reliable information and contacts and expanding consumer markets while at the same time curtailing the number of intermediaries necessary to do so requires constant adjustment—as does the work of the hinge. Displays of efficacy—in acquiring cheap goods and cheap transportation—often means sharing sourcing and distribution networks to retain visibility as a predominant player. Yet at the same time, Amadou always had to downplay his real capacity, lessen his chances of becoming a target of envy, so operations, inputs, contacts, names on businesses, statuses within various communities had always to be shifted, ever so slightly, but again imbuing everything with a sense of temporariness. Particularly as he tried to fulfill his obligations at home—something which he preferred

45

not to but could not reasonably circumvent—notoriety in his commercial endeavors invited unwelcome attention from bureaucrats and politicians always willing to arbitrarily invent or apply arcane regulations that always amounted to escalating shakedowns.

Amadou would go on to establish successful ventures in Bangkok, Guangzhou, Yiwa, and finally Mumbai, always staying a step ahead of crowded competition and repression of African entrepreneurship when it became too visible to its Asian "hosts." Always working the hinge, modulating visibility and invisibility, solidarity and multiple autonomies, money and spirit, Amadou demonstrates how the apparent parochial and baroque commercial ties long characterizing the economic life of the Futa precipitated wide-ranging prototypes for being African in the larger world. Filling containers in Guangzhou destined for various ports of call in West Africa were goods carefully curated to address the consumption needs of both aspiring elites and itinerant farmers in the backlands of the Sahel, as commerce was viewed as both solidifying existent lines of articulation and developing new ones. Amadou's forwarding companies in Dubai existed not only to circumvent constricted customs but also to host an often motley crew of Islamic students, young women workers staffing offices and hotels and on their own for the very first time, and adventurers without clear objectives. For commerce was to be a conduit of dispersed occupations, an unsettling of fixed expectations, all of which turned the cities he passed through into imaginary inventions.

Pan-Africanism here goes beyond political aspiration or the familiar tropes of solidarity. Rather, it functions as a surrounds in that it hinges itself on the multiplicity of more technical operations and strategic implantations across disparate terrains, using whatever means are available to engender connections, lines of stabilization, and flight. As something infrastructural, it is the culmination of many individuals like Amadou plying the world, never regarding a particular place as a definitive destination, yet never losing sight of all that the Chicagos of Conakry might very well be, right now.

For, the very designation of "Chicago" as the place where Amadou began his career in Conakry is itself a particular reading of the transversal. It is not only the appropriation of a name that connotes a collective recognition on the part of the neighborhood that urbanization in Conakry has become as politically messy and rough-hewn as implied in a stereotypical representation of Chicago now consumed at a distance. Rather, it is also a refusal to participate in a conventional naming of things that would most often portray Africans as ineligible for urban life and for the itineraries of Diallo to evidence the inability of urban residents to assume a stable life in place. Instead of representing an enlarging class of working poor, stuck in the margins at the heart of the city, without foreseeable prospects, and surviving within scores of petty activities, the designation of "Chicago" can be read as a conviction that their residence occurs within a "global city."

Far from Diallo's transversally elaborated livelihood being based as a compensation of an essential lack, it is rendered as the ordinary thing an emerging entrepreneur would do, given the fact that he resides in a "global city" where a local economy is elaborated through its articulation to a larger world.

While such transversal movements may long have been attributed to the cultural characteristics of the Fulbe, Diallo's insistence, as well as that of many of his "neighbors," that he pursued his particular livelihood on the basis of "coming from Chicago" turns this mobility away from cultural heritage to the ordinary machinery of urbanization in Conakry, a city most frequently viewed as an anomaly, as having a limited basis for existence outside of its history as a colonial entrepôt. At the same time, this invocation of ordinariness provides a cover for Koloma—the district's official name—to work out its own collective arrangements, livelihood practices, and forms of local institutions without accountability to the traditional trajectories of urban modernity. For "Chicago" must find renewed ways of reading itself with and against the grain in a context where infrastructural investments at scale are limited, and where urban social movements have often been forcibly suppressed.

So, in a twist of W. E. B. Du Bois's notion of the veil being the demarcation between white and Black life lived in the same city or country, in this story of Amadou, the public persona is itself a veil, driven by the contents of a project that remains inaccessible to all potential viewers, that manages to realize itself only indirectly, that never culminates in a single state or cultural imagination, that expresses its fate without capture.

Underground Railroad

It was only at the funeral for Amadou Diallo in 2018 that I met his youngest son, Fodio. As a result of his father's resources and his own intense drive, Fodio was a Wharton-trained economist who managed a major hedge fund in Paris. But in ways homologous to his father's project and practice, his was replete with utter determination and razor-sharp focus, but with a seemingly elusive objective. He made a great deal of money but claimed to own almost nothing. He styled himself to be less of a corporate player than a religiously possessed hip-hop artist. He nevertheless sat on several important policy

47

commissions advising governments and NGOs on issues of African migration and economic development. His name was spread across multiple boards of directors of various trusts and charities, and he knew the most arcane details of zoning regulations in some of the most obscure suburbs of Europe.

In 2019 I met Fodio in Castel Volturno, a small, infamous city just north of Naples. Here, he seemed to know just about everybody, from hardened thugs to voluble mayors to trafficked women to a large number of people seemingly just passing through. It was there that I learned, to an extent, of his probable involvement in an underground railroad, which focused on moving nearly indentured African farmworkers in Southern Italy across different cities of Western Europe in attempts to maximize their options for better lives. Before I get to more of Fodio's story and his fascination with the term *underground railroad*, I will take a brief detour into some of the historical uses of this notion.

The underground railroad is one of America's most enduring mythologies—an ever-recycled redemption narrative of collaboration among white abolitionists and runaway slaves, with the whites ushering the latter to "freedom" in Canada. In actuality, whatever "railroad" existed was a morass of fragments and usually ineffective sutures whose strategic efficacy paled in face of the more mundane and conventional "above-ground" modes of organizing resistance and contesting power (La Roche 2014; Haro and Coles 2019). The majority of successfully escaped slaves took alternate routes, either through the Caribbean or into the scores of maroon communities that existed within the terrains of Native America. Nevertheless, the underground railroad remains a critical instrument in amplifying the supposed reservoir of "good will" embodied in the American "spirit," evidence of a capacity to resist the dictates of prevailing law in the interest of emancipation.

In Colson Whitehead's (2016) novel *The Underground Railroad*, the metaphor is literalized into an actual underground rail service with a conductor and stations, albeit largely broken, and connecting destinations that represent a plausible counterhistorical reading. For example, there is an independent state of Carolina that had banned slavery but also did not permit Black people to live within its borders. There are feats of navigational prowess, community building, and inexplicably fortuitous encounters that give form to relations between geographies and peoples whose existence we might have always suspected but found difficult to map out empirically. Whitehead shows how the continuous interplays of confinement, interdiction, and fugitivity were literally shaped by the accumulated microresistances of Black people themselves. This literalization enables a detailed exploration of the landscapes of plausible dispositions, that is, the different ways America could have and might indeed look now if only the imaginations, sufferings, resistances, tribulations, and inventiveness of Black people would have been narrated differently—all that labor, generosity, persistence, and imagination that didn't have a language to express itself within.

My interest in this is not in the historical details or literary devices used to account for America's "original sin." Rather, I am interested in the underground railroad as a kind of speculative infrastructure, as a means of fabulation that generates a sense of uncertainty about how we read the present conditions of inhabitation. I am interested in it as a surrounds, or as a form of accompaniment to carceral infrastructures. In Whitehead's novel, the main protagonist, a young fugitive named Cora, repeatedly arrives at "strange destinations"—in one instance a massive "living history" museum where she finds temporary employment living out a series of revisionist depictions of world history. But she is constantly zigzagging across all directions, never availed the possibility of a direct, forward flight to any clearly designated "free place." In other words, in both spatial and temporal trajectories we are not on our way toward any destination that is capable of stabilizing itself as either good or bad for us. The sheer process of movement is always "shifting the goalposts"—that is, the valuation of what it means and implies as we, too, accumulate the residues of uncertain journeys.

Whitehead approximates our predominant condition of circulation, of circuits that both energize and exhaust. We keep on going because we are unable to get to the heart of any matter, and we therefore find it difficult to stop and say, "This is it" (even for now), while knowing that this leads to an exhaustion that may open new doors (but there are no guarantees). We can never control the terms of arrival, as Cora learns when she arrives at a farm in Indiana run by a free Black. When a member of his family worries that escaped slaves will jeopardize the operation, he ends up informing on Cora's presence, which leads to the entire farm being burned to the ground. We may find ourselves welcomed as refugees, contributors, but our presence always has untoward implications for some others. And then we are on the road again.

As a speculative or fabulous infrastructure, the underground railroad, perhaps, enables us to see how, materially, one instantiation of a built environment leads to another, but not in any seamless fashion as there will always be disjunctures, cul-de-sacs, interstices, and *terroir vague*. Rather, there is the possibility of envisioning the conduits that otherwise remain invisible when our cognitive attention is focused on the integrity of entities, or in our pursuit

49

of finding out "what things are." For example, in Italy's most popular television series, *Gomorrah*, set in Naples, underutilized, wasted, half-functional infrastructures are appropriated to assemble a system of illicit distribution, laundering, and storage. These infrastructures become an essential "character" of the show and point to the ways in which the metropolitan is made through a process of suturing and maneuvering across distinct types of spaces, of folding in different temporalities and rhythms of production into a totalizing machinic operation. Logistics generates its own vacancies and ruptures within which both the axioms of logistics and othering practices can be operative. While the violence of logistics is well-documented—the ways in which it disrupts ways of life and wounds physical landscapes and ecologies—notions of underground railroads also demonstrate the importance of retaining logistical sensibilities as a means of narrating the potentialities of collective life.

Fodio has waded into the murky seas of encampments, ghettos, and makeshift settlements that line the agribusiness processing zones across Southern Europe. These are areas of just-in-time, of field-to-shelf production, intersecting labor from Africa and Eastern Europe on short-term seasonal contracts, or often no contracts at all. These zones compress the aspirations of a better life with the freedom of corporate players to cheapen labor almost at will. As Irene Peano (2016, 2017) has exhaustively documented, the fraught crossings of Africans across the Mediterranean and their capture as exceedingly cheap labor by corporate agriculture become key elements of a lucrative business. Entire small cities take shape in abandoned military bases, warehouses, or factories surrounding tomato fields, replete with cheap services of all kinds for a transient population subject to constant racial abuse. Fodio's cousin, Ibrahima, an imam who lived in Turin for many years, became alarmed at the oppressive conditions in which African Muslims and non-Muslims found themselves and requested some financial help from the relatives in "Chicago" to assist.

As a result, Fodio spent many days sitting in dimly lit prayer rooms in Foggia, Cerignola, and Bovino listening to the stories of daily brutalities, of the violence directed against the very capacities of migrants to assess, to think, and to feel. Workers at various times had attempted to organize, strike, or put their case before a wider public, and they managed to win short-term concessions. But the collusion of foremen, factory owners, local politicians, and the mafia made it nearly impossible for workers to accrue any savings or to forge some kind of life outside of servitude.

Fodio knew that any formal interventions would be of limited use. After all, the Diallo family had built its substantial entrepreneurial capacity by traversing a multiplicity of back doors. So by forging articulations among stolen trucks and containers, hacked security systems, favors garnered from illegal Chinese factory owners whose relatives in Guinea moved large volumes of bauxite, and cooperation from networks of longtime Fulani residents in Milan and Toulouse with their own longtime connections to dirty cops and customs officials, Fodio began to piece together the semblance of an underground railroad. Along this railroad, willing residents of these plantation ghettos could keep moving and find a way to instantiate themselves in better situations.

Across the faceless, banal suburbs of Western Europe, Fodio's "charities" had already made investments in storage facilities, currency exchanges, parking garages, low-grade supermarkets, butcheries, repair shops, bakeries, car washes, day-care centers, and dilapidated but still viable apartment blocks through which circulated a world of discounted cargo destined for both licit and illicit consumption. A wide network of mosques and prayer halls cemented ties that, even though largely ethnically rooted, served as platforms from which to negotiate deals with Bengalis, Pakistanis, Kurds, Egyptians, Lebanese, and Palestinians who possessed specialized skills and assets. Fodio mobilized all this as an infrastructure through which the lowest of the low might pass temporarily. It is an infrastructure of more than bare life accumulation that migrants might pass through temporarily on their way to other destinations, back home or somewhere else in Europe.

Surrounding Detection

The underground railroad refers to how we might proactively rethink the terms of occupation, of situations whose trajectories are not clearly determinable now. This reiterates my long-term interest in the banal landscapes that Fodio engages as vectors of potentialities that are not predefined but activated only in the conversion of uses. Unlike the popular connotations of the underground railroad as an instrument enabling people to be "on their way to freedom," these potentialities of the banal, of all the seemingly faceless urban landscapes, are not dispositions to be uncovered by pulling back the veil of opacity. Rather, they concern the conjunction of imaginations with the capacities of receptivity embedded in the "host" (building or function). It is about how to read materials in a different way so that one can imagine

51

the possibility of operations capable of modulating their own visibility. It is about managing the inevitable necessity that everything that exists "announces" that existence in a particular way but recognizing, too, that there is no need, technically or morally, to "tell the truth" about that existence.

The underground railroad here does not hide the truth of its operations; it does not build trap doors, false bottoms, or moving bookcases. Rather, it finds ways to infuse all the operations we might take for granted—the cheap restaurants, bakeries, convenience stores, warehouses, storage spaces, and parking lots—with the capacity to "do their job," function as normally as possible so that all kinds of other functions might be embedded within them. It plays off the assumptions, for example, about what "diasporic" business is supposed to look like. As Fodio emphasizes, "We are not asking for them to change their 'stripes,' to be something that they are not, but rather that eating, baking, storing, parking and so forth could be so much more than what we know." It is about imagining the capacity of the apparently banal to fold in actors and practices that are not normatively envisioned as part of their purview.

Detection now plays an increasingly important role in our lives. Especially during the time of the COVID-19 pandemic, the capacity to move, circulate, restore familiar patterns of work and sociality depended on the capacities to detect the presence of viruses, to detect trajectories of transmission and surges and the flattening of curves. The ways in which the focus on maximizing the interoperability among surveillance technologies and data sets constitutes specific objects and bodies and posits continuously reformulated designations of danger and threat from the search for emergent patterning derived from multiplying the angles and forms of observation are well documented (Browne 2016; Amoore and Raley 2017; Amoore 2018).

But there are also other more minor or subtle matters of concern when it comes to detection. These are about not only how present conditions are read in terms of detecting trends and patterns, but also about the ways in which people detect themselves in a cascade of reports, stories, and analyses. How they see themselves as a part of or apart from particular renditions of reality. There are those, for example, who detected that the COVID-19 pandemic crisis was a definitive crisis, that from which the once normal can never be restored, the harbinger of a new world and economic system. There are those who experience this time more cyclically, who detect the return of conditions that they already experienced some time ago, that reset the game and that wipe out all the activisms and efforts of decades or a generation.

For example, many progressive activists who have worked with poor communities and social justice issues detected in the early pandemic conditions a return to 1998 and the end of the New Order regime of Suharto. On the one hand, all the work that had been done to strengthen the capacities and livelihoods of low-income settlements, to build new civil institutions, appeared to have been largely undone in a matter of weeks. On the other hand, decades of activism in India aimed at making the state assume more responsibility for ensuring the social welfare of the majority suddenly materialized in a substantial program of food and income support—but in a context where many of the intended beneficiaries had, at least momentarily, disappeared from view. The practices of opacity that enabled many to secure livelihoods under the radar now complicated the ability of the state to reach them. Here, detection became an intricate game: the need to be fed but also the need to avoid capture.

These conundrums are set within a larger game of contestation about ultimate values—the exigency to live versus the exigency to be free—reducing detection to all kinds of exhausted binaries or at least to arguments about *proportionality*. What proportionalities are proper for what kinds of populations? Should those whose livelihoods are dependent on day labor, hawking, waste recycling, artisanal factories, and marketing be forced into more extremes of impoverishment in the interest of reducing infection and morbidity rates? What degree of enforcement of spatial restrictions constitutes heavy-handedness?

Recipes for disaster would suggest a proportionality of ingredients, as would the rectification of disasters. In other words, genealogies are a matter of deliberating what proportion of an event can be attributed to chance, planning, or the respective contributions of economic, cultural, and social factors. If Black and Latinx households are more vulnerable to certain conditions, what proportion of that vulnerability is due to the residual traumas of racism or the compensations applied; how much is attributable to personal behavior, to the stresses incumbent in living as Black, or to the institutional deficiencies that are a byproduct of racialized provisioning. Of course, all these dimensions are interconnected. But we live in a time when the calculation of proportions is given great importance simply because of the focus on interconnections. By opening up causation to a multiplicity of variables, and by making distinct sources of data as interoperable and translatable as possible, the emphasis on proportionality becomes the basis from which to develop policy and programmatic interventions.

But what if proportionality were neither evident nor possible? What if it were unclear the extent to which realities on the ground were at the same time self-destructive, virtuous, frivolous, necessary, generous, and manipulative? What if it were impossible to tell exactly what is virtuous or debilitating?

In such instances, everything becomes experimental, heuristic, a wager on a particular disposition. Detection stretches to enfold nearly impossible calculations as to the likelihood of viral transmissions in urban settlements that are difficult to lock down, where interactions between exposures to various outsides, circuits of mobility, probability of contacts with those engaged in foreign travel, access to the tools of prevention, such as soap and water, are estimated as probabilities according to differing proportionalities of contributing variables (Isin and Ruppert 2020; Leclercq-Vandelannoitte and Aroles 2020).

There is thus a need to rethink the practice of *detection*. Currently we find ourselves obsessed with the need for better detection. In the growing contestation between the preservation of life for all (another mythology) and the exigency of restoring the economy, new modes of detection and discrimination came to the fore. Some nations, for example, emphasized the need to massively roll out COVID-19 antibody tests to determine the extent of existing immunity to the virus so that those who are immune might be permitted to resume "normal" activity and thus reactivate economies. Here, access to circulation and the resources that ensue from circulation are guaranteed to those who are immune, while those who continue to be at risk were to be circumscribed to operate within various modalities of confinement and detachment.

Given that metabolic rifts, feral effects, and species-crossing pathogens are likely to produce wide-ranging pandemics in the future, genetic composition may be the only truth that counts, and one subject to the protocols and efficacy of the testing process. It is possible to imagine scenarios that extend the neoliberal surveillance preoccupation with *preemption* to the identification of a wide range of future biological (and neurological) risks (Pellizzoni 2020). Other extensions might include the probable existence of viral agents produced as an aspect of the Anthropocene, and then individuals might be tested to determine their probable risk factors and inherent susceptibilities to these agents. How likely is it that particular individuals and populations embody genetic dispositions (in addition to environmental factors and personal histories) that carry specific risk factors and therefore warrant specific circuits of legislated movement? These regimens of preemption are added onto already existing forms of racial and ethnic profiling and are extended through the use of new technologies of phenotype identification, such as tentacularity, to create entire suspect populations (M'charek 2013, 2020).

Standard forms of detection always assume a truth that is to be uncovered, even if what is detected exceeds the existing terms of understanding. Something *needs* to be known. So it is not so much a matter of whether the truth uncovered is the truth as whether the self-confidence of detection generates sufficient reason to reiterate itself as the definitive method for establishing the basis for decision. In contrast, Rob Coley (2020) draws on the classic film noir, where the detective is less interested in the "real story" than in trying to work out the unanticipated complications that the pursuit of the mystery has unwittingly thrown up. Detection here seeks less to uncover complicity and conspiracies than to detach itself from the accruing story. It is more interested in the tactics of ensuring that things do not come to light. For to understand the crime to be solved means seeing how the crime has permeated into all aspects of living and how the transparency of detection might leave nothing in its wake. Such an approach draws on François Laruelle's (2013) notions of *generic* detection, where the objective is not to find the relations among things, not to put together all the clues and variables into a sufficient explanation, but to stay with insufficiency. This is a necessary aspect of underground railroads as speculative infrastructure.

While it is important to emphasize those dimensions that envision the ways in which one thing leads to another, all the unrepresented articulations of spaces and times, it is also important to step out of and suspend a unilateral focus on relations. This is what the generic does: it breaks the possibility of detection being the method through which individuals and populations are subsumed into a system of proportionality—more or less healthy, more or less immune, more or less eligible, more or less valuable. Instead, the generic connotes a space or composition capable of holding within it things and processes that may be related to each other, or not—where what something is may be multiple but does not owe its existence to how it is positioned within a network of multiplicities and through which it accorded particular statuses and potentialities. It is impossible to tell what the generic is for sure; there is no way to affirm the value of a particular instance of it except in terms of indicating what *it is not*.

While Alex Galloway (2014, 31) may succinctly render the generic as "essentially, nothing, or as close to nothing as it is possible to be while still remaining 'something,'" it is important to always explore what that "something" is—something that can never be taken for granted and that is the occasion for continuous observation. Just because "the generic is a negative universalism that is indifferent to the difference of ontogenetic flux, a lived immanence that precedes difference and refuses to ontologize the real," does not mean that it is static, a kind of dead weight of constant refusal. Here both the no/thing and some/thing operate as a kind of ruse. It is difficult to tell just what all is compressed into the generic. The identity of the components may be clear. But the extent to which they are operative, and to what

55

Without Capture

degree, remains uncertain. As such, relations of power—and thus subjugation and subjecthood—also remain uncertain, as any explanation escapes from the terms in which it is framed.

In my own investigations of the massive housing complex in Jakarta where I once lived—twenty-two towers, each with twenty-two floors—I spent several years attempting to determine how this complex was actually administered and what was *really* going on in terms of its social composition and legal standing. On the surface, Kalibata City seemed like just another faceless example of affordable mass housing, with its tiny, cheaply constructed flats almost all sold before completion. The complex differed from scores of others in Jakarta by foregoing the inclusion of integrated parking structures in favor of ground-floor commercial shops, laundries, eating places, and social service facilities, thus creating the semblance of a typical neighborhood. Originally intended as a stepping stone for young aspirant middle-class families, Kalibata housed a vast array of household types and individuals of various sexual and religious orientations across flats that could be owner-occupied but that were more likely to be subject to endless subletting. Flats were leased from the hour, the day, the week, to open-ended futures. Flats became parts of the portfolios of scores of "brokers," who would trade control of them for "rights" to manage parking, delivery services, sex rings, and religious schooling. The terms of everyday inhabitation were literally all over the place, seemingly controlled by the absolute "sovereignty" of Kalibata's developer, which had the formal right, if not the actual ability, to regulate all official governmental administration and access. So many games and transactions were compressed within this generic built environment that almost any story one might want to tell about it could conceivably be true. Trying to get to the bottom of things proved to be a useless endeavor, and this was not just a matter of faulty methodology.

Rather, the construction of continuity, the sheer ability of Kalibata to keep going can be attributable only to a continuous rearranging of the proportionalities of all the different kinds of practices—both on and off "the books"—that informed the fiscal, infrastructural, material, and management operations of the complex. Rents, fees, loan repayments, and salaries may have been steadily paid every month; repairs were made, security enforced, supplies delivered, and waste evacuated; but the precise ways in which these were accomplished seemed always to depend on a process of constant adjustment. At the same time, residents rarely believed that they resided in some fundamental mystery and rather, for the most part, relished the prospect that whoever they were and whatever they were doing could be "written into" the complex. What

1.4 | Kalibata City, Jakarta. Photograph by the author.

would normally be registered as potentially implosive situations, where the social antagonisms among different kinds of identities, tenancies, affordances, and costs would diminish stability, actually engendered a sense of people "being in the same boat." While developers across Jakarta rush to label their products with an exciting brand, Kalibata residents often, in a typically cynical Jakartan style, referred to the complex as *biasa aja*, as just something that "is," without any special features at all, as close to nothing as something can be.

So the underground railroad is also a way of being a detective who discovers within his or her "beat" a "real," that is, "this one, right now, right here," which has no definitive connection to anything else. But by doing so, such detection levels the playing field and renders something no more or less important than anything else and thus avails it to unthought of (so far) courses of action. One could see detective work as a form of rendering, of making things (up), of making something available to a particular (wider) use, of putting things into people's hands, things that they didn't have before

57

or couldn't imagine using. Less an uncovering than a rendering, detection, then, is a way of keeping things moving along, of telling stories that extend a person's relationship with the world rather than being the grounds to legitimate the removal of persons from worlds.

These considerations are also close to specific Fanonian strands of Black thought, as David Marriott (2018, 225) indicates when he renders Frantz Fanon's concept of blackness as the "unnamable event of an infinite postponement . . . the structure of a never-having had, because it never has had an Other to ensure it." Even if Marriott is wrong about the unnamable—for blackness is named here—the thought, nevertheless, says something important about the underground railroad not having a destination called "freedom," but rather being movement that proceeds without the coordinates of escape or arrival. Marriott's "never-having had" is not merely a case of an absence, nor is it a matter of a self-invention that reproduces the terms of recognition that accord to oneself the value that had been denied. It is not a matter of experiencing the loss that is compensated for by assimilating the categories of self-valuation that had been used to deprive Black persons of the status of being human. It is not a matter of writing oneself into history or of obtaining the freedom to constitute the terms of one's own existence. For that was a "bad trick" all along—a trick in the sense that no matter how aspirational and accomplished those once wretched can be, the proof of their ability simply reiterates the function of the terms that marginalized them in the first place. No matter how transgressive or excessive the performance of a self-conscious blackness might be, the versatility of such excess—even a matter of "pure matter"—is thinkable only through the available forms that calculate excess as such.

Rather than loss, as Fanon (2011) points out, the wretched are an infection at the heart of colonialism, but an infection that, while being localized, is also *immune to definitive detection*. It is immune because the wretched reflect both the versatility and the violence of representational systems—because the wretched have a capacity to offer an account of that which would seem beyond their capacities. At the same time, these representational systems count on the wretched to offer themselves up as the necessary surfeit of meaning(lessness) that enables the recalibration of colonial orders. Of course, the wretched are neither no/thing nor one thing. We may come to think that we definitely know who the wretched are, that somehow the term is able to synthesize the specificities of, for example, Melanesians of Papua, the Siddi of Pakistan, the Chorotega of Nicaragua, or the Geechie of the Carolinas, and how they got to be "wretched." But in using this as a generic form, a vast set of experiences, maneuvers, and circumventions have been at work that make the wretched more than victims, more than their appearance. As such, their generic rendering does not so much reduce them to a single meaning or form as hold within that form so many different implications and potentials that have been forgotten but that can also operate in service of the wretched forgetting the need to commit to any singular appearance. This simultaneous supercharging of detection and its limits is what Fanon identifies as the ground for a range of aporetic effects, the possibilities of invention. We will come back to this in chapter 2.

While, as Achille Mbembe (2013) indicates, there may now be a generalization of the wretched across all conventional categories of discrimination, and while viruses, toxins, and CO_2 levels become the "real" wretched, there is still something worth retaining about the human as the wretched of the earth. If the time of the earth, according to Dipesh Chakrabarty (2019), is a temporality beyond the comprehension of human discourse, the earth's wretched posit a mode of human existence that is most removed from the practices of mastery that increasingly render the earth uninhabitable. A "return" to the earth could just as easily mean the materiality of death as it could signal a renewed inhabitation at a "safe distance." By a safe distance, I mean not an intensified integration with earth processes, as is the popular message of ecological politics, but rather a generative detachment from the position whereby humans destructively interfere with earth processes. For what are the wretched to do when they are no longer that?

When in 2020 all the workers streamed out from big Indian cities by foot on their way home without money or prospects, what did they plan to do when they got there, if they got there, besides wait for the all-clear signal to return? What if they were not to return? What might they have considered if they were then to "shelter in place"? In some Mumbai districts, petty traders took whatever wares they had to sell to the rooftops, servicing the demand for goods issued from below. What will happen to a refiguring of the street if these traders decide not to return to the "ground"? If hundreds of thousands of "slumdwellers" do not "make it" through this epidemic, what kind of "ground" will be produced across the now-empty tenements and shacks?

If the wretched endure, it is not clear what that endurance will mean or bring. But that endurance potentiates a necessary distancing from the earth as a source of endless material speculation and logistical proficiency. It will require thousands of off-grid experiments, new forms of gathering up essential nutrients across extended circulations, and provisional settlements. The wretched pose the question of a fundamental need to refigure the notion of what it means to inhabit—of how households are organized, of how eating, sleeping, fucking, caring, and making are to proceed in a world of limited liquidity and rising sea levels. Where will this take place, and how? The multifaceted domains organized here as the *refrain* of the surrounds point to tentative places where abolition is being prefigured. Whatever new governance arrangements are put in place to save the world, the wretched will remain partly removed, somewhere in the surrounds, and in this removal, they will provide the workforce for restituting all those "wretched places" scattered across the earth.

Chapter One

TWO

FORGETTING BEING FORGOTTEN

It's nation time eye ime
it's nation ti eye ime
chant with bells and drum
it's nation time
—Amiri Baraka, "It's Nation Time"

In the first chapter, I talked about a series of spatial practices that navigate the treacherous interstices within and beyond capture, something I posit as the surrounds. I emphasized the "not yet beyond," for as Zakiyyah Iman Jackson (2015) reminds us, the calls for a beyond too often ignore praxes of humanity and critiques produced by Black people, particularly those who are irreverent to the normative production of the human or illegible within the terms of its logic. In this chapter, I look at the surrounds as a way of doing time, something I designate as the "forgetting being forgotten."

Once upon a Time in Papua

Sorong is the largest urban area in West Papua, Indonesia's most eastern province. It is the gateway to what is considered one of the world's most spectacular tourist areas, Raja Ampat, and is the administrative center of what is emerging as one of the largest zones of low-carbon extraction, replete with lithium, nickel, cobalt, magnesium, and rare earth metals. Sorong is also situated in one of today's most militarily repressed, thoroughly colonized regions, where the Indonesian state has long done anything necessary to suppress the aspirations of indigenous Papuans for national liberation. This was an aspiration dutifully expressed according to international law in 1962 but one that failed in its realization due to the political mechanizations of cold war politics that saw the United Nations succumb to complicity among the governments of the United States, the Netherlands, and Indonesia in deterring the supposed spread of communism (Kirksey 2012; Viartasiwi 2018).

In the past decades, West Papua has largely been forgotten by the international community, particularly as its indigenous inhabitants are too often viewed as "stuck in time," both incapable of and disinterested in managing their own nation. Possessing the earth's most diverse biosphere and, until recently, remaining largely unnavigable by road, West Papua was far too removed to warrant much interest beyond those with the capital to exploit its riches. Nevertheless, a plethora of resistance movements have endured over the years; small groups of armed insurgents have operated in the interior highlands for decades, sporadically making their presence felt. Continuous generations of young students have constantly challenged the Indonesian encroachment on everything—land, family, and culture (MacLeod 2015; Slama and Munro 2015).

Indigenous Papuans are now a minority population in the face of the inward migration of minorities from other East Indonesian provinces who have insinuated themselves in the transport and retail sectors, and in the face of the heavily subsidized mass transmigrations of rural dwellers from Java who have been promised large tracts of cheap land (Haluk 2017). Large-scale corporate agriculture and mining have forced many Papuans into the major urban areas. In Sorong, this has meant increasingly difficult interchanges between the native Moi, who retain customary authority over large swathes of now urban land, and the nascent demands of incoming Papuans from other regions, who are claiming space and opportunities under the auspices of a still aspirant national identity whose institutional platforms are constantly being eviscerated by the operations of the Indonesian military.

Because of Sorong's position within long-standing circuits of trade, the Moi are widely viewed as the "worldliest" and the least Black of Papuans, and there is a common joke that for each Moi household it is an embarrassment if there are any fewer than two university graduates, a man and a woman (Suaib and Fitriana 2015). Sorong is a rambling town dispersed along a north-south axis of some seventy-five kilometers. Its centers of administration and economic development have rapidly been transferred from the old center and its ports and markets, farther south, toward its massive petrochemical installations and the zones primarily populated by immigrants from Java. It is one of Indonesia's most cosmopolitan cities in demography if not always in atmosphere, and it is the largest constellation of a so-called Black Melanesian population. It is largely Christian, in contrast to the majoritarian Muslim identification of Indonesia, and comprises residents from Ambon, Northern Sulawesi, Kei, Arawak Islands, and Nusa Tenggara Timur (Surya 2016, Webb-Gannon, Webb, and Solis 2018).

These so-called other Blacks from neighboring provinces bring with them particular skills and orientations cultivated by their original locales and the colonially shaped expressions they were allowed to take: ex-fighters, brawlers, drivers, thieves, mechanics, tricksters, marketeers, and seafarers. The solidity of any consolidation of ethnicities and regionalisms into a "Black identity" waxes and wanes, shows up and dissipates according to the situation or place at hand and who and what is being contrasted or enjoined (Tirtosudarno 2018). Sorong also possesses an overwhelmingly youthful population, and schools, churches, mosques, and clubs are teeming with different experiments, with words, performances, sensibilities, and tensions.

Police and military personnel are everywhere, but many are in plain clothes and function also as land brokers, financial consultants, engineers, loan sharks, development planners, and religious advisors. While a nominal local-rule policy is in place, which assigns at least on paper the bulk of civil service jobs to the Moi, their sources of autonomous income, as well as their regulatory authority, are limited in an always delicate dance between plying the administration as the ticket to economic advancement and using their positions to cushion the intensity of state violence (Syailendra 2016).

At the very heart of the old urban core, right behind the city's sprawling main market, is a wide expanse of semiforested land, nearly resembling a classic city park, verdant and rambling, which is the traditional home of one Moi affinal grouping and now primarily settled by a loosely knit network of Rastafarians, hip-hop artists, hustlers, civil servants, layabouts, fisherman, and cultivators. Some come from households with a fair amount of money; others have always been dirt-poor. The grounds consist of all types of makeshift constructions—shacks, huts, three-story wooden apartment blocks, simple bamboo shelters, and more elaborate edifices constructed from shell and discarded materials. In the last instance, the land is inalienable, as this is officially *adat* land, cemented to the use of whatever lineage can legitimately display connection to the MoiKaron subclan to which this area was formally

63

ceded (Kusumaryati 2020). While the Moi have been dispossessed of most of their customary holdings, this expanse at perhaps one of the most strategic locations in the city has largely been forgotten since, as one Javanese taxi driver put it, "They are not interested in developing themselves. . . . They have not only forgotten the significant education that Indonesia provided them, they have forgotten the industriousness and the ways of life of their ancestors; they simply lay about, scavenging and thieving."

One of the ironies of the area is that it is both widely accessible and impenetrable at the same time. The "community" if you want to call it that has helped build a walkway along the inlets from the sea that are plied by longboats carrying goods and passengers from outlying islands to the center of the market. From this walkway much of the interior of the area is visible, open, yet still recessed, not because it is foreboding but because it is such an anomaly in the larger surroundings. Just a short distance across the inlet at the northern boundary is a typical rickety and overcrowded neighborhood of the Bugis, the traditional seafarers, whose density of cultivated dilapidation stands in stark contrast to the near pastoral setting of Peppemaranda. Lambert, an artisan who fashions bamboo beds sold in the nearby market, claims, "We have everything we need: we store rainwater, we make compost-based sanitation systems, we have every food we might desire."

Indeed, residents were always tinkering with things, as well as leaving things alone. Wilson, a man with an unspecified occupation and who grew up in faraway Waina, talked about the district as being a place of "spontaneous combustion." Many elders had gone elsewhere to concrete houses on demarcated plots with cars, leaving the young ones to manage, which they did by rendering all kinds of people extended family. Their wheeling and dealings with each other about responsibilities and rights sometimes led to prolonged arguments, even violence; but such conflict seemed always to have been resolved by rearranging things—space, household compositions, and tasks—as no one was that interested in taking charge of anything except their own singular rhythms and pastimes. Lambert said that any dispute was always easily forgotten, as was the assignation of specific authority and tasks to specific individuals. Things happened, as Wilson claimed, in "their own time." What was particularly important in the residents' ethos was the sense that they could largely live as they wanted because the city had forgotten them. Perhaps this was partially true, for indeed the potential value of this land, given its location and size, was always being concretely depreciated in the frustration of scores of developers more than willing to pull out the big bucks, the political clout, and deep reserves of deviousness to take hold of this property.

First, those to whom the land was ceded and entrusted fell in the gaps between different branches of the Moi that had gone their own way. On top of this, countless numbers of bureaucrats always seemed to forget where essential documents had been deposited. In efforts to go around negotiations with customary Moi authorities, surveyors would often inexplicably forget to bring certain equipment, key actors would forget to show up at meetings, incoming municipal administrations would forget what the previous ones had decided, and litigants would forget to file the essential paperwork. This meshwork of forgetting buttressed the reputation of Peppemaranda as a place of "no good." Inhabited by residents deemed incapable of making anything useful happen, the area accreted layer upon layer of attributions that any project would likely and quickly face its own demise.

But it was not only a matter of being forgotten. For the residents were not interested in any kind of recognition of their efforts, rights, or endurance. The claim of being forgotten was always accompanied by the invocation that they themselves had *forgotten about being forgotten*; that it did not matter to them; that they were, as Lambert put it, "called upon" for other purposes—although who had called and for what objective was also something forgotten. There was simply a call that came through the sudden twisting of leaves in a vegetable garden, or the piercing sounds of cicadas in the trees, or in the sudden appearance of a small child having momentarily turned completely pale, or in a frail woman sitting in silence on a porch after having walked seven straight days from the hill country. One could respond or not, and there was no sense about how adequate the response might be to the objectives intended by the call, for each call could quickly change its mind in terms of what it might want from the person to whom it was issued.

Wilson indicated that such calls never came at the "right time," that even if they were expected, there was something unruly and surprising about when they actually turned up. There was no time that was the right time, and so Peppemaranda did not so much live according to rights (or wrongs) as according to exigencies, the sense that something needed to be done right now; but whether it was actually done or not didn't seem to matter. You could forget about it; there would be more calls, more inexhaustible opportunities.

Time and forgetting seem inextricably entangled, when time is experienced, if not measured, in terms of a play of forgetfulness rather than of memory. So, the game of time is to be forgotten, to forget that one is forgotten, to forget that being forgotten matters, and to forget to respond to a call whose objectives, implications, and terms of fulfillment are themselves forgotten. I have encountered this notion of being forgotten elsewhere; it is not

65

unfamiliar. In Omdurman in Sudan, I lived next to a neighborhood that was self-designated, "We are the dogs that God forgot," as if the very possibilities of memory were rooted in human residents converting themselves into a companion, yet less valued, species that was then forgotten by the only entity that possesses the capacity, even duty, to remember everything.

At the outskirts of Nouakchott in Mauritania, Haratin, descendants of former slaves, have recently constructed a shantytown, which they commonly refer to as the area "we have already forgotten." When asked about the reason for this titling, residents claim that they have even forgotten why they had done so: "We have already forgotten." Perhaps what was forgotten was the lingering trauma of oppression, the constant ways in which the Mauritanian state continued to exclude what was now the majority of the nation's largest city from any significant participation in its political and institutional life. Perhaps, as some reluctant residents ventured, the term referred to the desire of residents to not pay attention to where they had come from; that the whole purpose of this place was to start anew. Others offered a more radical version, claiming that the title referred to the forgetting of who they were or are, a refusal of any of the features through which they were to be identified: "We have already forgotten who we are." For common precepts that link the possibility of forward action to the necessity of remembering where one came from, of who one is in terms of some core identity, this emphasis on forgetting is a seeming reversal of this equation, a desire to live on but in terms fundamentally unrecognizable to any familiar framework of interpretation.

In Kinshasa, I once knew a youth gang, one of the many Bloods affiliates in the city, that filled an empty warehouse with found objects and documents of all kinds gathered from trash bins across the city. Gang members said these items would be used as evidence in a popular tribunal that would eventually judge the merits of whether the residents of the city would be entitled to remain. If the judges they claimed had been recruited from the wretched (their word) across the continent found the residents guilty, the residents would be condemned to a temporary exodus from the city, only to return to their same places and lives, but having forgotten anything about them.

When I asked "51," the main protagonist of this story, how such a judgment would be enforced, he indicated that it would be the women who would respond to the call, the call to leave, and the call to return. Why women? I asked, to which he replied, "Because it will be the time of women, for only they can recognize the call because for so long they have called upon each other. They have called upon each other to manage almost every aspect of life."

As he explained:

You have to remember that men are simply accountants; they add and subtract; they tell stories about who did what to whom; they invent all kinds of excuses to justify their not being able to do anything really important. They make judgments; measure whose dick is bigger; invent all kinds of rules for avoiding tending the garden, bringing in and cooking the food; they invent memory as some grand story that excuses them from doing any real work, tales of heroes, and major accomplishments. Only the women are capable of forgetting; forgetting about how their work is forgotten; forgetting all the times where they alone have had to keep things going; forgetting their own dreams so that their mothers are not forgotten. They will understand the call; they will know what to do; they know how to live when everything is forgotten.

Time as "Taking Care"

What kind of time is this? In the Cliff Notes version of the well-known Prometheus myth, Epimetheus, the brother, is called on by the gods to imbue each creature with an overarching defining quality that would forever institutionalize their inhabitation of the earth and their relationships with other creatures. The only problem here is that Epimetheus forgot to assign the human a definitive character. Perhaps, he still fantasized, mourned, or even believed that humans remained essentially citizens in the pantheon of gods—despite their actual removal. Whatever the reason, Prometheus, responding to the urgency of humans prospectively wandering the earth, lost and aimless, broke into the vulcanizer's workshop of the Gods and stole the fire that was bestowed on them. Fire became the essential technical apparatus through which humans could constitute their own evolutionary emplacement. Here humans were bestowed that volatile, energizing instrument, unstable and always in need of tending, through which the image and capacities of the human would be produced.

As compensation for being forgotten, humans were provided the apparatus that enabled their conceit that the world would never again forget them. Instead of being constrained by a definitive set of capacities, features, and scope, technicity would enable continuous anticipation and adaptation to new circumstances, the ability even to enroll those capacities of other creatures for the specific ends of man. Technicity itself was to be the locus of memory, as every tool and apparatus would double as an archive of what was possible, and

67

through their own actions, humans would generate trajectories of new possibilities (Stiegler 1998). They would figure a narrative arc, a history that could be brought to bear on the very shaping of human capacity and governance.

Of course, humans could well forget, as the by now trite injunction "Those who forget the past are condemned to repeat it" points out—as if forgetfulness itself embodies stasis, a frozen time, or a time without time. But the artifices and systems of retention inevitably delimit human capacity as well, reduce the complexity of human relations with the world (Stiegler 2009). For as much philosophical thought has emphasized, time is disjuncture, difference, and breach.

Ezekiel, one of the residents of Peppemaranda, would constantly play the old Chambers Brothers classic, "now the time has come, no place to run . . . time has come today," as if time were responding to a call. It has now arrived, and there is no place else to go, besides here—even as Lester Chambers announces that he has no place to stay and dreams of the subway but can't put off the call to another day. Everything is to be forgotten in order to answer the call, because the call demands an answer that cannot be prepared for, just as in the familiar invocation of the "call of Islam": who one is and what one has done can never be sufficient preparation to respond to a call that has inexplicably been directed to you out of millions of potential recipients.

In this formulation I am aware that I am skirting the generative work of Bernard Stiegler, who has persuasively argued the extent to which the capacities of thought and action are contingent on what he calls the *extrosomatic*—those technical systems of tertiary retention that bring with them the edited experiences of the past as instruments that shape what it is in the present that we are likely to pay attention to and remember (Stiegler 1998). And these systems are not simply retentive, but protentive as well, for they posit specific incipient forms for imagining the future, of anticipating what indeed could be retained at some future point (Stiegler 2010a). While forgetting remains an ethical dilemma, an orientation among the different registers of retention that entails a necessary turning away from, or refusal to bring about, the implications of forgetting seem already anticipated, in that we always come into a frame in which attention is inevitably tied to the past (Stiegler 2010b).

Nevertheless, in contrast to the move toward entropy of the functioning of any system—its tendencies to fall, dissipate, atrophy in the repetition of the ways in which it organizes its constituent elements—Steigler posits a different economy, whereby energy actually increases through the very iterations of a narrative, storyline, or performance that has lured us into paying attention and which inexplicably results in something else besides the normative, something that *forgets* to dissipate or decay (Stiegler 2018). Far from calculative logics of understanding that attempt to identify precisely the probability of something occurring, of narrowing the horizons to mathematical finitude, the materialization of thought as incantation, as call, as bearing witness, what Bernard Stiegler (2010a) identifies as *a taking care* can generate the improbable—something that forgets its likely impossibility.

In this time of the Anthropocene we are constantly reminded that time is running out, and probably has already run out. The long histories of propping up human life as an always self-aggregating and insatiably voracious consumer of the efforts of other forms of life and nonlife, even to the extent of converting some humans into the exemplar and legitimation of what could be wasted and exploited, have finally been caught up in some vicious feedback loop to undermine the very possibilities of ongoing existence. Here humans are called on to do something that might transform not only their own possible extinction but all the multiple extinctions that result from the human standing bare and alone in front of a world of new toxins, viruses, bacteria, and chemical alterations.

This call, while seemingly definitive and urgent, is a call for difference, for complexity, for abolition—a call to participate in the changing of everything, for it is everything that issues that call. But instead of responding to the call by forgetting all that has come before, by forgetting that all of what one is can never be adequate to the invitation the call makes, humans too often simply reiterate their name and emphasize the exigency that humans must be saved at all costs. All the sufferings and constraints experienced by specific humans, particularly those whose humanity has indeed been largely forgotten, must now be truly forgotten in prioritizing the very survival of a species that has really never lived as a species.

But in the end, it is the apparatus that must be sustained, that which associates the human with a capacity of reason, intelligence, and science—a very partial aspect of human experience. But this intelligence has always been a gathering up of different forces, materials, sensations, and practices that do not belong properly to the human (Colebrook 2019). Each gathering up has freed up space within the locus of the human body to do other things with what it has—space where ability and dominance are simply one set of features generated through the very encounter of bodies, things, and forces with each other, each momentarily stabilized in specific territories of operation within specific milieus or surrounds (Povinelli 2012).

Deploying the notion of the human as some kind of fundamental explanation and frame does little to capture the complexities of such gatherings and what might ensue from them. Quranic verses are full of indications of how the oneness of the earth is constituted through the multiplicity of inscriptions, of a world full of signs not provided by Allah but by the earth itself. This is a constant process of this thing leading to another, a broken branch leading to a leaping monkey, leading to birds emptying from the trees, descending on a farmer's field, alerting the occupants nearby, and so on and so forth (Kohn 2013). Calls can be issued from anywhere and transmitted along long lines of signifying chains, or they can simply appear as if out of nowhere. These are not calls for the survival of a particular formation of the human. They do not limit the human to a single form, still predominately imagined as white and male.

As Claire Colebrook (2020, 377–78) has repeatedly pointed out, rather than refuse any concept of human nature and insist that we can always become other than what "we" are, we might see "human nature" as a formation that exists in ways that are far more complex (and embedded in the earth) than capitalism because now what thinks of itself as humanity no longer claims to be some divine essence, not even a universal norm, but a procedure of maximizing potentiality. This can occur at a microlevel, where the twenty-first century is no longer a soul-searching journey of discovering who one is but is a matter of day-to-day self-management, intensifying what one might become.

Here, the exigency to never be forgotten impels a narrowing of the horizon of what the human actually is. In the desperate attempt to not have their existence forgotten, the human-technical complex that retains the evidence of an ongoing drama of accumulation by any means necessary as compensation for the dread of being born with nothing at all holds onto to all the slights, deficiencies, triumphs, and catastrophes as proof of an essential resilience. It thus forgets that the long history of being forgotten situates the human within complex gatherings within the earth, which can be renewed and transformed. Forgetting that one has been forgotten means forgetting the human as some kind of transcendent signifier.

Just in Time

Forgetting can also be deployed to leap-frog over certain kinds of gatherings. Gatherings that accrue things over time, that would seem to specify any disposition as a product of linear developments, where a led to b and thus c. Slowly, over time, through discernible increments and stages, a scenario or event is construed as the culmination of some continuous buildup, a progressive gathering of materials and forces. But forgetting can cut through such a process and enable persons to show up and intervene at specific moments without having paid attention to all the incremental deliberations that resulted in that present state of affairs.

The predominant orientation to justice would seem to suggest that eventually suffering will be redeemed, that through time, as time goes on, there will be a working out of everything that went wrong in the past; that *in* time itself, is the promise of a more just life, a rebalancing of the forces, and the promise that all forces tend toward a final balancing. Then there is *just-in-time* production, where things are made and delivered just when they are needed. Circumventing the requirements of costly inventories and permanent labor forces, the just-in-time promises a synchronous lining up of availability and need. Here, linear progression, a building up of supplies that will be available in sufficient quantity to both address needs to come and create them as well is partially replaced with operations of instantaneity that would seemingly overcome time. Particularly within contemporary imaginations of logistics, this matching of a "just situation" with a friction-free rendering of what is desired detracts from a sense of justice to be found in a process of historical eventuality marked by struggle and strategic planning.

The just-in-time also posits another possible reading. Here, no matter what has transpired, no matter the disproportions and inequities, there can be, at a single fortuitous moment, a different kind of reckoning based on a calculation that does not so much ignore the discernible trajectories and increments as rework them according to an eventful mathematics that re-gathers them in unprecedented ways (Meillassoux 2011). No matter how things appear as a particular set of arrangements and predictable outcomes, justice can be affected through a reading that interrupts the seemingly proper place and distribution of that which is gathered. Such alternate propositions may not alter the fundamental structural positions of the materials gathered in time. But time and time again, such a reading and the subsequent interventions it informs can be reapplied, albeit in a different way, with different outcomes.

Here the just-in-time occurs at that moment when particular dispositions, results, and judgments seem irrevocable, edging past a tipping point. But then in just *this time*, and no other, an intervention occurs that restores faith in the ordinary ways in which those gathered normatively conduct their business, something that is neither inside nor outside the setting, where a more equitable distribution of opportunity is affected. Everything that occurred up until now is momentarily forgotten, as are all the slights, wounds, and resentments, as whatever one has managed to hold onto is given new

71

purpose. A call has come from somewhere, just in the nick of time. Let me illustrate this in an ethnographic vignette from Kinshasa.

Kasa-Vubu, a quarter named after one of the Democratic Republic of Congo's most prominent political leaders, had been developed as a combined commercial-residential area just on the other side of the southern limits of the former colonial enclave. Its advantageous location enabled it to develop a cosmopolitan edge, reflected in the various backgrounds of its traders and residents. The commercial area has been redeveloped several times, but each time such effort seems to invite more overuse and overcrowding. The surrounding residential areas have some of the highest levels of population density in the city and are places of rough conditions and rough characters.

For a crew of guys I know in Kasa-Vubu, it is hard to tell when the work really begins, or what it really is. The most intense activity seems to occur in the late afternoon in a crisscross of various satisfactions and apprehensions. There are some traders who are relieved to have made more than they had anticipated and who look forward to treating their friends to a beer. There are others who have barely sold or made anything and who are reluctant to return home. There are those who will hide from creditors and those who will under-invoice the day's receipts. There are those who will attempt to bundle what they have left with the surpluses of others and who see if they can quickly pass off the package deal to those who roam the markets at this hour looking for last-minute bargains.

Cedric, Lumanu, Makoto, Bazana, and Armando are the titular heads of the Bloods in Kasa-Vubu. With their red bandanas they have styled themselves around the American gang, and indeed they are well informed of its histories, personalities, and organizational structure. The K-V crew intends less to be a "branch" of a global organization than to appropriate certain "themes" and ways of operating to insinuate themselves into the local economy. With the exception of Makoto, all are university graduates, and their grooming and eyewear convey "young professional" rather than "thug." They all occupy a parcel of land left to Armando when his family unexpectedly departed for Europe without informing him. He needed to recruit his present "associates" in order to hold onto the land in the face of competing and aggressive claims from kin.

The crew spreads across the nearby Marché Gambela at the start of the trading day. They canvas the initial expectations—for a market is a field of affective textures, from indifference to driven urgency—and these forces compel an array of discursive tactics and deals. Given the decaying infrastructure of the market and the various clogs of the transport routes in which it is embedded, the trading day must also circumvent incessant delays—from gridlocked traffic to the wait for deliveries, the goods that are set aside for pick-ups that are slow in coming, the sporadic supplies of electricity, and the unanticipated arguments that are not resolved quickly.

As marketing entails getting what one has access to out into the largest conceivable world of consumers willing to pay a good price, trading concerns the opening up of vistas of sight and perspective. It entails what the trader can actually see, but also what they can anticipate, what they imagine to be taking place beyond the immediate field of vision. To a large extent this is what the Bloods deal in. At the outset of the day, they try to get a sense of what the market anticipates, in all its various individuated and grouped sensibilities of how the market "feels" about how it is situated in a larger context of events.

With the swirling of hopes, anxieties, exigencies, and indifferences, each trader in the market interferes with the capacities of others. Whether crowding in or stepping away, each trader shapes the spaces of transaction, for it makes little sense in an overcrowded arena of small transactions to simply wait for customers. There is the need to circulate, to round up possible sales, to make certain products, services, and prices readily available to someone whose intention was only to acquire a specific good and not others, and to convince them of an essential "conviviality" among discrepant items. While it is true that some traders stay still in the recesses of this mobility as a means of offering discretion and limited visibility, Gambela is a stage for showing cards for those who mostly do not hold them but who are convinced that once they are about to trade hands they know enough about where they are to make them appear almost immediately.

For the Bloods it is a matter of trying to assess how the traders they deal with think about their location at the start of the day—that is, is this the day they have to pay off the big Lebanese creditors; is this the day that wives will collect from their *tontine*; is this the day that groups of buyers will come in from the distant suburbs beyond the airport. Then, traders in the market are rarely alone; they belong somewhere; and in Gambela there are the West Africans, who have been in this market for generations; there are traders with special affiliations to Chinese, Lebanese, or Indian wholesalers or brokers, who can mobilize credit and connections to facilitate supply and advantageous prices.

There are those who walk in various uniforms, and in the market the uniform tends to obscure rather than clarify representation as many try to

73

invoke an authority from somewhere. There are traders linked to big politicians, and others linked to churches or to growers and brokers from provinces from which come the bulk of specific goods. In the efforts of traders to put together an expansive vantage point—that is, a plane along which they can envision a ramifying series of events and people to whom to articulate what they have access to—the actions of others in the market assume a fundamentally ambiguous position, for they can both block and facilitate, elucidate and dissimulate.

In a city of intense scarcity and constantly shifting belongings, where there are limited numbers of games and resources to work with, success is often a matter of slowing others down to allow one the time to get to some piece of information, some money, some customer before others have a chance. This means throwing up detours and deviations. At the same time, straight paths, while often enabling speed, have their own limitations. For when people are forced into deviations and circular paths, they have the possibility of paying attention to scenes and people they otherwise would not think twice about, and in these encounters they discover unforeseen possibilities. Here, regardless of the spatialization entailed, a straight path will mean little if the person is unable or unwilling to move fast, and the circuitous path will mean little for those unable to be patient enough to take in the view. All these factors are the "materials" that the Bloods will work with.

But at the beginning of the day, they simply try to "take it in," get a sense of the intensity of aspirations, the willingness of certain traders to assume various ways of seeing and figuring, and the way that the market is "coming together" through the interactions of transport, goods, stalls, affects, and openings. They spend no more than an hour at this, and then they go back to sleep, as if the dreams, if there are any, will become an important modality for designing what they will attempt later. The crew will return to Gambela in the late afternoon, just as things are both winding down and thus speeding up. It is a time when the tendency to desperately try to unload, to make some money, is at its peak. This feeling intersects with the accruing patience of those who feel they have done as well as possible, and that it is important to sit tight and not make any mistakes, not to go out on any limb. It is a time when the market is also most a mess. Not simply because it has been worked all day, and the mess is a sign of that work. But also because traders have been holding goods for others, bundles may have been proposed but are not going anywhere, and things now have to be disentangled, returned to their proper places. But just as they are on their way back, something else may intervene to convince them of still other possible last-minute destinations.

This is one facet of what the Bloods do. They wait until the last minute and try to force through different kinds of "alliances" between these goods on "their way back." Given what they observed in the morning—the various assessments of location, the different moods and expectations, the different opening prices and bottom lines—the question for them is where are these sentiments, expectations, and assessments now, now that the trading day is almost at a close.

Additionally, no matter how much a trader has made at the end of the day, the reality remains that they owe something to someone—creditors, family members, fellow traders, patrons. They need not be paid today, but at least in the abstract something must be set aside. But what the Bloods do is "suggest," and sometimes "compel," this extra to be put into play, so as to help fund a last-minute purchase; help cover an urgent debt in return for a favorable volume of a certain good or service; join in a collective purchase of a service, such as protection, expedited delivery, or circumvention of tax or duty; or help fund someone who is travelling and who has a good jump on a favorable price of some bulk purchase. Of most traders, who are never satisfied with the day's sales, who claim that the city has forgotten them, that customers fail to remember the good services that they have been offered, the Bloods ask that they forget this being forgotten; that at the end of the day, just in time, new attachments will emerge.

Because the Bloods have nothing easily discernible to buy or sell, they devote all their attention to reading the potential willingness of traders to engage in actions they would not otherwise consider, and to reading the sense of how traders think they are connected, not only to each other but to wider scenarios. For example, relations between Lebanese wholesalers and Gambela retailers are often fraught with tensions, particularly when the wholesalers hoard supplies or hold the traders captive with extortionate prices. Then, the Bloods identify ways to try and "go backdoor." Here they might arrange thefts from warehouses, or make sure that a wholesaler's kid goes missing for a few days, or capture a competitor's wife in some compromising position, or spread rumors about how certain big merchants are holding back on payoffs to their guys in the government.

While reluctant to use violence, they find it necessary to maintain a reputation for violence as a kind of guarantor for an authority to be exerted in a market that cannot rely simply on threat or extortion. For at the end of the day, the task is to work with the loose ends, to concretize potential futures from what is left over, not as the only horizon, but to use the task of working with leftovers as a means of reconfiguring relations within the market and beyond. Cajoling, seducing, steering, and sometimes pushing different actors forward to gain each other's attention, the Bloods will "suggest" ways of packaging leftover food, some recently arrived bundles of clothes, and diverted electronics that didn't quite find their way to the expected pick-up. These packages could then head toward a van on its way to a mega-prayer meeting in nearby Matete, and then park near a bevy of food sellers in an attempt to catch the pre- and postmeeting multitudes.

As everyone rushes from the market into the crowded thoroughfares and minivans and buses, a Blood or two will be making sure that certain vehicles are able to jump the queue, as long as the drivers are willing to make room on their rooftops for a few bags of cement delivered for free to a group of construction workers willing to do a few hours of underpaid overtime at a trader's little satellite shop in the suburbs in return for a connection he has with the ministry handling a big project in Gombé. The rules and norms are forgotten as their transgression is forgotten as well in the immediacy of new arrangements.

The end of the day also requires impression management. The appearance of success is critical. Traders will often mask their desperation and insist on certain prices until the end. But this adamant attitude can also be thrown into the mix; it can hedge those who want to get rid of something for almost any price because they need something for the dinner table that night. The work of the Bloods is to bring together the divergence of expectations, desperation, and patience, as well as those who think long and short, those who see far and wide or only the immediate area around their stall. The "today I will do for you, if you will do this tomorrow" is founded on these very discrepancies. For there will be those who can wait a month to be paid, or two months, because they see the fluctuations in the supply chain and know that they can afford to have someone hold something now—a good, a price, a service—because they know its value will be markedly different later on. There are those who know that a few weeks from now, a client or a potential customer will probably need a certain quantity of an item just when supply is constrained and thus are willing to acquire it now and hold on. Then there are those who are willing to take a chance on an item or class of goods that they would not have considered before but can now easily acquire and simply put into play as an instrument to affect the price of something they really want.

For the Bloods, work is the choreography of these intersections and exchanges. What counts, first and foremost, is extricating a good or a service from the use and value that is anticipated for it at the beginning of the day and then seeing, later on, the extent to which this "hold," this association between a good and its framing, has been maintained, and whether there is now flexibility to dislodge the equations that link trader, good, price, and use and thus set other connections in motion. Again, there are goods that are left over, those that arrive late or never come, those that come in the wrong quantities or are delivered into the wrong hands. There is spillage and scarcity; things that had circulated during the day, trying to assume advantageous locations and bundles, that are now on their way back to their "proper" owners.

The Bloods attempt to link materials such as food, wire, cement, cloth, hardware, and pharmaceuticals regardless of the common significations of their use. They are simply things that are making a particular last-minute appearance/disappearance in the market. The objective is to interrupt the flows normally suggested by their marketing to carve out transactions that may have little to do with how many actual or potential customers there may be for a particular type of commodity, either now or tomorrow. These normal regimens are to be forgotten.

This practice follows from the recognition that, clear or not, useful or useless, urban bodies are entangled with such collections of materials. For many, habitation takes place in environments where the inputs for producing life have no consistent supply chain or vehicles of evacuation. Bodies are intimately entwined with scrap, fuel, rain, heat, waste, sweat, tin, fire, fumes, noise, voices, and odor, on the one hand, and in multiple stories, generosities, violence, arguments, reciprocities, and fantasies, on the other. There is no bringing all this into a single account, into a predictable means of calculating opportunities and reasonable futures. This is the kind of implicit recognition that the Bloods work with, sensing that at the end of the trading day it is perhaps impossible to draw up a viable account, and then using that as the basis for speculating on other possible outcomes.

Of course, all these materials in circulation belong to someone, have actual or potential value to someone. They are someone's property and possibility. Things are not easily dissociable from these significations. Once held, and then exchanged, it is not always clear under what conditions they can be replenished. In a city where the institutions of mediation are weak, claims to authority suspect, and predictable trajectories of input and output usually provisional, there can appear to be little room for maneuvering.

Such conditions would seem to emphasize the need for steadfastness, trust, and stringent codes of reliability. These characteristics are certainly on display in the market. At the same time, in a city where individuals try to implicate themselves in the lives of others and where performing consistently in any endeavor is fraught with unforeseen contingencies, since people are weakly anchored in ongoing institutional roles, keeping goods and services within strict parameters of specific uses is difficult and often not in people's best interests. Things have to be converted into unexpected uses and values in order to keep them moving and to use that movement to maximize a person's exposure to a wider playing field.

So it is possible to attribute all this maneuvering to the structural conditions of uncertainty that pervade almost all aspects of Kinshasa's life. This is an uncertainty that compels residents to hold on tightly to family ties, long-cultivated economic arrangements, and procedures for assuring some measure of trust. While these solidities certainly endure, they become the default position, the basic "grammatical" moves for launching what Yves Citton (2016) has called diagonal positions, where new collective forms of agency are always being devised that both engender and "solve" uncertainty through finding ways to gather up and articulate the singularities of desires, inclinations, and a readiness to "make moves" with principles of equal respect needed to mobilize not oppressive strength in numbers. Uncertainty is instrumentalized as a strategic strength rather than a structural vulnerability; as such, uncertainty becomes a cultivated uneasiness about how the necessary calculations of efficacy are to be made and then addressed not with certain standardized repertoires of cure or problem alleviation but with equally uncertain, momentary arrangements addressing how that uncertainty might best lead to a disposition that need not be protected or institutionalized in the long run, but that works, just for now.

As such, the Bloods can be seen as purveyors of a surrounds, offering a form of accompaniment to the normative procedures of a market that operates, just in time, through the multiple gaps and interstices that come and go depending on changing conditions and the time of day. Using the circulation of objects, infused as they are with various intensities of expectation and guile, as a means of piecing together relationships that promise, if never guarantee, a widening of the field of vision, the Bloods activate a series of exchanges and articulations that are always incumbent in the organizing logics of the market itself—its operational surrounds. The "promise" is that the trader can have access to contacts and experiences they otherwise may not encounter, and the first step is to forget the particular sentiments and calculations with which they have previously approached the things that pass through their hands. Such opportunities ensue only if they can let go of the particular meaning that these things have and let them exert their own forcefulness—and to forget that they themselves are doing this forgetting. For if one insists on making this a self-conscious choice, it becomes just another "market strategy." This is why the Bloods swoop down on the market in the way they do, as actors from elsewhere, free to give voice to what the goods themselves seem to want. At the same time, things are imbued with specific, highly valued meanings, and this disjunction between memory and forgetting is not something to be reconciled or negotiated. Instead it produces volatility, a moment when things could go in many different directions; it is this volatility that the Bloods attempt to both provoke and steer.

The Bloods can only do the work they do—trying to put things into play, trying to use them as instruments to bring different scenarios and actors into an unanticipated proximity—because they don't care about, and have indeed forgotten about, what these things mean. While they may be bearers of intensities of expectation, disappointment, need, and imagination, these sentiments are important to the Bloods only because they signal a difference from something else, some other sentiments and uses, which then open up an opportunity for a deal, a deal in articulation. No one seems to remember the Bloods or anything that they have done. They are simply part of the surrounding background, and they don't strive to be anything else. They are content with their good works being forgotten.

While I only really skim the surface here of complex microeconomies, what I am trying to illustrate is the importance of broadening the usual notions of livelihood. Livelihood as a domain and problem has been too often reduced to considerations of employment, business, or discernible production activities. It is about the amassing and deployment of material resources and money, usually in terms that refer to the effective management of households. But livelihood also seems to concern a field of maneuverability, the acts of creating spaces where living can be exercised and deployed. Life seeks to enhance its ongoingness and stability by producing conditions that bring its critical details into view and that minimize the uncertainties inherent in the stretching of its capacities. The increasing complexities and aggrandizements necessary to secure life can undermine its largely improvised efficacy.

These operations in the market, performed repeatedly, as much as they can be, also act as ways of taking things apart. Some of the things taken apart are long-established relationships and organizations that persist, but with increasingly varied half-lives. What the Bloods do is neither liberatory or redemptive. It doesn't mean that they change the rules of the game. If what the Bloods attempt to do is to circumvent the effects that actors and things have in the market according to particular redundant arrangements, the stuff of the market is also catapulted or returned to a different phase of existence.

Things are not necessarily transformed but are instead rendered in form, making them available to different calculations and sometimes simply to the highest bidder. Perhaps what in the end the Bloods represent is a capacity to experience and read the intricate choreographies of inclinations and maneuvers that are positioned to emerge, that are embedded in all the mundane procedures of greeting, setting up, transacting, and dealing that populate the market but that require a series of lures, prompts, and provocations to be unleashed. This results in a chain of events that is difficult to predict and calculate, but that in many ways makes the market: that density of goods, services, impressions, circuits, commodity chains, and rituals that can settle into predictable routines but that are also always surrounded by unexpected lines of connection. These lines are possible not as planned outcomes but instead exist just in a specific time—in this instance, just as trading is winding down and still informed by a palimpsest of imaginations with which the day began.

This is the ongoing problem of the Bloods' forgetting and their emphasis on the turbulent just-in-time rearrangement. Such orientations will always constitute a limitation on the productivity of experimentation, for it comes to devalue certain hard-won accomplishments of consistency. It could problematically signal that all that has been accomplished through negotiations and practice over years can be simply superseded by an experimental moment, the just-in-time, and that the problems of legitimacy and available resources in the larger society authorize experimentation for its own sake (McFarlane 2007; Lindell 2010; Mahon and Macdonald 2010). This is then why the Bloods do not merely intervene when they feel like it. It is why, except for Sundays, they never take a day off. What they do is never accidental, and through their constant labor, they seek to be a valued infrastructural aspect of the market, even though everyone else may forget that they are.

In Kasa-Vubu, the Bloods have no job, official position, or discernible future. After the time I spent with them, I am not even sure how in the end they get paid. They have money, but not in large amounts. They exert some kind of authority, but it is not clear exactly what. Sometimes what they do works; more often they are laughed at or met with complete indifference. They are a highly visible presence in the quarter, but only for short spurts of time. They never socialize locally and are apprehensive about being too exposed. Some are wanted for crimes and make a big deal about avoiding the police; but at other times they couldn't seem to care less. Clearly a particular kind of force field is being played here in the ebbs and flows of intersecting ambitions, constraints, claims, losses, hopes, calculations, tactics, impressions, and manipulations. When I returned some years later to look for them, no one seemed to have any idea of whom I was looking for. Kinshasa is a city full of tricks and deceptions as well as grinding boredom and limited options. How speech, dress, words, gestures, timing, speculation, reading, and intuition are deployed become critical aspects of livelihood—of making a surrounds for life, a place, a cover, and a performance that interweaves with various instantiations and expressions of living in order to move it somewhere else, if only for the time being.

Time's Gathering, or the Fullness of Time Forgotten

As pointed out in the first chapter, there is not only *this world*, but *this* place, *this* gathering, *this* time, none of which can be generalized. The *thisness* is not static or frozen, but continuous, enfolding, and unfolding. Michel Serres (1997) talks about time as a topological process, a matter of switched gears, downstreams suddenly diverting upstream; of someone being suddenly fired up, losing their head; of the magnetisms of touch, of innumerable vibrations and churnings that constantly interrupt the possibility of an invariant background against which to measure a definitive progression. Yet, within this chaos, there is also the work of things being prolonged, endured. This is particularly important, as Elizabeth Povinelli (2016) points out, because of the ways in which an *ancestral present*, always attuned to the necessity of innovation and recalibration in the coconstitution of life and nonlife, continues to be reified and frozen through colonial mechanisms of extraction. These mechanisms treat the *ancestral present* as ancient history, as stuck in specific cultural beliefs and practices ill-suited to the development of the modern world, a development that requires the extraction of those very forms of nonlife through which that ancestral present maintained itself as a dynamic, embodied system of inhabitation.

Relegating that present to a sedentary past thus not only legitimates the exploitation of nonlife. It also abstracts what is considered to be nonliving from a larger context of cosmological functioning where the boundaries of the living and nonliving are either shifting all the time or fundamentally ambiguous in terms of how forces, entities, and materials are gathered and interwoven with each other. Karen Barad's (2007) notion of *agential realism* is also significant here in its recognition of interstitial objects, an intermediary mode between what could strictly be demarcated as life and nonlife, which is referred to as the *inhuman*. These are apparatuses that can sense things beyond the cognitive capacities of human perception and the specific secondary

81

qualities exuded by objects. It is this realm of the inhuman that also introduces new complexities to the gatherings mentioned earlier.

Similarly, Mark Hansen (2014) refers to a worldly materiality that implicates human life in ways that go beyond the confines of the body. Here, digital media do not simply operate on the basis of the specific intentions communicated by human agency but rather that human agency is shaped within digital and calculative circuits, constituting a plane of operations that is not organized in terms of human and nonhuman, life or nonlife, self or other. Rather, as Brian Massumi (2017) points out, these circuits recursively incorporate the feelings generated by this immersion into crisscrossing data streams into specific embodiments of observation, of attending to the surrounds, that exceed the conventional vehicles of sensing or its distribution into the perceptible and imperceptible.

The call, which I have talked about throughout this chapter, is issued from potentially everywhere, and it is one to which potentially everything can respond, even though this may never be the case. It will elicit a panoply of strange responses and affiliations, even as they take place somewhere specific, with their own forces, characteristics, energies, and constraints. This impulsion to gathering reduced not to likeliness, desire, or necessity but rather to what things can do simply because they can is the incipient indication of a surrounds, a precursor to the concretization of specific territories with their functions, infrastructures, and demographics.

For as Deleuze and Guattari (2013) point out, any territory emerges out of a multiplicity of milieus. They use the example of the ocean, where the energy of the sun, the forces of current, the nature of water, osmotic membranes, schools of fish, sand and geological formations—in other words, multiple milieus—operate in ways that crisscross each other. These crisscrosses become dimensions, inscriptions, definitions of the territory, expressing the territory as a specific consolidation of different kinds of forces and registering the notion of place and function. Yet, these things are not the territory itself.

In the urban surrounds, then, we are not talking about a resilient population, neither a flexibility of human agency nor the intersections of informalities. Rather, territories of operation are formed through the forgetting of past functions and definitions, even as bodies, infrastructures, materials, and atmospheres retain in their very constitution the entirety of experiences of a past. Steven Shaviro (2003) reminds us that in cities, roads, buildings, pipes, wires, animals, viruses, and humans feel each other out, and this process is conjoined as more than one and less than two. Each folds the other in without being completely subsumed. The time of the now, this instant, is the

2.1 | What time forgot. Photograph by Michele Lancione.

time of forgetting, even as that instant is itself long forgotten in the progression of future forgetting. Things are no longer what they were nor are they congealed into what they will be. Forgetting goes backward and forward and back again.

This doesn't mean that one forgets everything. That somehow forgetting avails a free, frictionless, logistical paradise where we can get on with everything because we carry nothing on our backs. There will be those who will rightly refuse to forget what has happened to them, because such forgetting would give free rein to the acts of oppression committed against them. Also forgetting can be faked, where the pragmatics of survival require accommodations that modify what is to be publicly remembered. In many respects it is harder to forget than to remember, especially as everything seems to count more. In environments where there is so much to pay attention to that might in the end be relevant in terms of individuals curating more efficient and potentially profitable performances, it is difficult to put together hierarchies of relevance, to assess what is more or less important than anything else (Citton 2014). Simon Lilley and Dimitris Papadopoulos (2014) argue that every tangible or intangible object or activity can be potentially valued. But the realization of such value requires apparatuses of calculation, comparison, and assessment that enable different objects and experiences to be mutually translated, thus ensuring a comparability of values—in what Lilley and Papadopoulos call a technology of temporality. Here, value is sustained by technologies that basically steal the future by imposing meanings on it in advance. Still, this theft is often contingent on the simultaneous enactment of different kinds of times that clash, cooperate, converge, and diverge to muddy the waters of how value is produced and defined.

In the literally muddy waters of the Hooghly River in West Bengal, Laura Bear (2015) has conducted ethnographies that explore how workers, bosses, investors, municipal authorities, unions, and thugs duck and dive with and through each other to modulate the very being of the river, as well as the ships and cargos that flow across it. The different rhythms of engagement with the river generate different approaches to valuation, what Bear refers to as ethics.

Contrasting emphases on steering ships through increasingly compromised waters, keeping employment going, extracting as much value from transshipment as possible, and converting port lands into high-end residential developments all bring together different practices and temporalities that can obscure the interdependencies involved and render the critical issues those of national and ecological regeneration, as if the two could not exist without the other.

> State employees described their work as a historical, nationalist duty grounded in care for the goddess Ma Ganga and for rebuilding a sonar Bangla (golden Bengal) lost at partition. They feared the corrosive forces of Muslims, the private sector and informalised workers. It was the benevolent state alone that could achieve the public good. River pilots asserted a historic heroic duty of care for each other, inventing new technical devices to fix the contradictions of accidents on the river. Private entrepreneurs emphasized their future-oriented flexibility and adaptability to the transcendent force of capital. They grounded this in Hindu principles of dutiful service and the productivity of a divine nature. Anti-productive forces for them were the state and unionised workforces. (Bear 2017, 149)

Here, what is forgotten are not only the real forces of diminished labor and exploitation at work and the assault on the very intimacies of everyday social life of those inhabiting the river's banks. There is also a forgetting that the viability of the river simply cannot accommodate the dominant assertions of the uses made of it. It is a forgetting of the very things that the river is and of the kinds of forces that sustain it. But, at the same time, it is also perhaps necessary to forget that it must be saved. For, the remembrance of the imperative to save always reiterates the very same consciousness of the primacy of the human operator neglecting their proper place in the dynamics of riverine ebbs and flows. Here, the river might "choose" to forget being forgotten, wary of all the technologies of redemption waiting in the wings.

Not dissimilarly, the imagination of friction-free logistical movements obscures the extent to which moving things around is a gathering of disjointed techniques and operations. The pursuit of smooth interoperable relations and seamless integration pays insufficient attention to all the frictions, chokepoints, and discrepant practices that are at work in assembling goods, transporting, and offloading them. As Mike Gregson and his collaborators (2017) remind us, in order for cargo to move, it must be gathered up. Things have to be arranged in their proper place so as to be properly contained in order to move across designated spaces. Goods have to be assembled in warehouses, placed into containers that are consolidated in vertical stacks according to specific units of measure, loaded onto ships, offloaded from these vessels into ground transport, inspected, and then broken down into units that will be wholesaled and retailed.

All these processes are conventionally subject to different uses of software and protocols of calculation and, depending on their location in the port system, are also managed by different companies. The result is a kludge of protocols and technicities that are never optimal but that seem to work for now, until the time when they don't. Here, while the purveyors of logistical imaginaries forget the messy labor relations and technical practices necessary to keep circulation going, those who do the "dirty work" forget this being forgotten in order to come up with often makeshift, improvised ways of connecting their piece of the commodity chain to the others.

Such logistical operations reflect the seemingly contingent nature of things and the ways in which contingency is enfolded into the very basis of what is valuable or not. As Martijn Konings (2018) asserts, the purposeful creation of uncertainty and insecurity can be an important resource for economic actors attempting to buttress their positions by claiming a capacity to roll with the punches. Uncertainty can be a fundamental aspect of any new deal. As such, contingency is always a move toward taking things apart, the formation of a new rubric of explanation, and a way of intersecting discrepant materials and positions within new alliances with new capacities of self-reference. Such moves further amplify and individuate contingency, since the implications of these new alliances cannot be fully visualized in terms of the viewpoints of the alliances themselves.

In this vein, Ben Anderson's (2015, 2017) work on emergencies suggests a time that instills a sense of forgetting that we have, perhaps, been in a particular place or condition before. Whereas other past emergencies have either

85

been quelled or been debilitative, we, nevertheless, remain now in the face of further emergencies. But what he also emphasizes is the endurance of an emergency time that simply does not go away, that does not have a prior temporality of normality to return to. He calls this the becoming indistinct of the endemic and eventual, the structural and impactful. Here emergencies are prolonged beyond the now, but in themselves they constitute a seemingly endless now that has no infrastructural support to be forgotten, a kind of long, slow death that never resolves itself either in the end or in the amelioration of its fundamental condition.

For so long, the apparatuses of colonial and racial domination have purposely been oblivious to the suffering they cultivate. In part, obliviousness to this suffering is possible when it becomes the by-product of turning bodies into cheap labor and moving them around at will. Here, suffering accomplishes something by maximizing the accumulation of the few, of producing one new thing after another. In some contexts, suffering has constituted the basis for providing healthcare and insurance, or it has served as the legitimation for relief, or emergency and development interventions. But suffering also remains as its own outcome, because in many respects it is simply useless. It cannot be folded into any other product, destination, or time. It is an endless now that is forgotten because it leaves traces everywhere and finds no apparent use except its own expression.

Condemnation to early, slow, protracted death in the face of systemic abandonment derives as much from its uselessness as from its utility. In dispossession without accumulation (Abourahme 2018), where the act is entirely self-referential, lives are undermined simply because they can be, at any time or place, not necessarily without implication, but without any need to keep something in reserve or to compile reserves. And this aspect of dispossessing without accumulating can be largely forgotten in the emphasis on the albeit distorted generativity of racial capital. While there has been voluminous academic work demonstrating the ways in which Black enslavement and oppression is at the heart of modernity, this work also functions as an instrument of forgetting—forgetting the sheer uselessness of such a history. Here, abolition is in part a politics of active forgetting in order to affirm the singular procedures of sheer cruelty—that something can be done in this place (any place) in this time (any time) just because it can.

In an atmosphere that prioritizes the right and imperative to remember and to name, the forgetting of being forgotten may seem unduly pessimistic, ethically irresponsible. Again, the invocation of the generic is important here as that tricky "something" that offers itself up as nothing in (the) particular.

Because it is more than a stripped down, minimalist position; it is instead a compression of many things that remain undetectable in terms of their individual identities. The generic posits the possibility that within erasure—of position, subjectivity, and memory—there is mobility, maneuverability not tied to the established coordinates. Something does get named; something does seem to connect to a past, but with the generic, it could be anything.

To certain people at certain times, to forget having been forgotten may be an integral aspect of the possibilities to discover and enunciate aspects of this human and this world that open both up to important crisscrosses of things, to calls coming from here to there, which enable the formation of a surrounds. This would be a surrounds both in the sense of the debilitating images and apparatuses of racialized control being surrounded, "Come out with your hands up," or alternately, "Put your hands up in the air and shake them like you just don't care," and providing a space of temporary unfettered, experimental operations in the midst of apparent capture.

Methods for Unsettling Time

Between extinction and abolition, not as fixed goal posts but rather as oscillating realities that play off each other, it is possible to think the space of the surrounds. It is both a place on the way and the experience of being on the way. To further flesh out what might be seen as the time of the surrounds, I want to draw on three "methodologies" from critical Black American thought, a Senegalese manifestation of Afrofuturism, and a Jakartan rendering of Michel Foucault's notion of a life that is other, as five exemplars of particular ways of thinking through the conundrums of forgetfulness that go beyond simply forgetting in order to remember, or remembering in order to forget. These exemplars are *invention, fungibility, malpractice, Set Setal* (Be clean), and *exposure* as they relate to the instantiation of a particular kind of time. While the three methods, drawn from what is often referred to as the "great American Black conversation," on the surface may seem to confirm a pessimistic dimension to the forgetting being forgotten, I deploy them not as philosophical conclusions but as experimental tools to *detourné* seemingly impossible constraints into possible openings of maneuver.

There has been a tendency for Black thought generated by the American experience to stand in as a global depiction of blackness and in ways that do not usefully resonate with the diverse experiences of Black people in the rest of the world, even as they, too, have been subjected to various instantiations

87

2.2 | The availability and opacity of method. Photograph by Michele Lancione.

of racial exclusion. It is not so much that any invocation of a common blackness is empirically or psychologically inaccurate as it is that distinct historical
positions and territories of operation lend opportunities to surround apparatuses of capture and captivation with different punctuations and inflection
to elaborate that very commonality, that very genericity of blackness, with
constantly changing proportionalities of sentiments, languages, demeanors,
dissimulations, cynicisms, and hopes instead of being reduced to a single
position—whether social death or ineluctable joy. This is reflected in Sharad
Chari's (2017) meditations on the biopolitical struggles of Black residents
living on chemically toxic grounds in Wentworth, Durban, which asks us
to listen to what is being born, not only barely survived. Instead of any ontological constancy that grounds suffering as default position, Chari's invocation of the blues as an aesthetic of spectral refiguring continuously shifts
around questions of the bearers, uses, and implications of suffering, of those
capable of performing life with an intensity beyond any modality of capture.

Here the diasporic circulations of the blues act as a practice of "speculative
futurism" for those who know that capital's phantom objectivity is always
spectral, unable to secure any viable form of life but "without a melancholic

critique stuck in racial repetition and cultural difference" (167). Thus, the American "tools" deployed here are meant to "turn the corner" just before they might reach any obvious conclusion, to traverse the most seemingly arduous landscapes of confinement only to reach the possibility of further inquisitiveness, curiosity, or what *might be* when all the expected oppositions appear exhausted.

INVENTION

With invention, I am indebted to the work of David Marriott (2018) on Frantz Fanon's notions in this regard, although I offer a rather heretical, oversimplistic, and unpessimistic interpretation. Fanon's preoccupation is with what might constitute a real break from the debilitating narratives that constitute not only the discourses of colonial imposition but the very terms of self-regard on the part of the oppressed. The overturning of the colonial regime is insufficient in terms of really forgetting the mark it has left on the bodies and psyches of those it ruled.

A breakthrough, breaking the chains of command, the alignments of forces, or penetrating into the supposed heart of state power is not enough to unlock those capacities of a human that were long suppressed. For any enunciation of them, any display of abilities beyond the confines of the human as it was enforced, were to always be punctuated by an asterisk, a qualification, indicating that any creative manifestation inevitably had to take into consideration the status of the oppressed as the condition that colored it. Black thought, no matter how singular, was always to be "blackened" by its inability to break through to the other side of liberation. Thus, anything creative would also be testament to the enduring power of the colonial, its seeming imperviousness to countermapping and counterdiscourse.

As Fanon (2008) indicates, breakthroughs tend to retain the need for the very codes and practices of narration that are broken in order to really demonstrate, or at least confirm, that the breakthrough has indeed occurred. So even if the answer to that colonial history from the other side of liberation might be that of rearranged interlocutors and altered speaking positions, that answer inevitably takes the form of a reiteration—before I was not free, now I am free; yesterday you made the rules, now I make the rules—where reversals are marked, but the normative language of attainment has not been forgotten. Instead, Fanon demands a future imperfect, a time that never arrives, never stops arriving, the destination that cannot be foreseen, only a process repeatedly traveled, a territory to be invented.

The future here is not a standpoint, not a measure from which the distance from oppression can be read or a time in excess of any preceding continuities. The wretched of the earth are not simply wretched in terms of their status within the colony but in their own volitional and involuntary refusal to imagine or declare a time of redemption. They have already forgotten what ails them; they have already forgotten that their lack of income, education, status, and self-comportment disqualifies them from really contributing anything to this world, let alone a new one. Their capacity is one of being able to operate in concert within their own terms, within their own inclinations toward each other. Each of them knows exactly what to do with each other without having to institute a body that defines the valences of possible dispositions. They need no mirrors for their collective efficacy, no image of a conjoined body, for it is invented in their very trembling, tentative, half-baked leanings toward each other; it is all the incipient gatherings that shatter and scatter coherent viewpoints.

Such invention is necessary because, as Fanon (2008) reiterates, a "real" individual is deemed a subject through their initiative and development. But such has been foreclosed to Black people because, first and foremost, the Black is regarded in terms of a characterization that does not belong to them but that, no matter what they do, becomes their inevitable destiny. But such a trajectory is denied at the level of the ideology of rule and in accord with the principles and epistemologies of the colonizer who, after all, has undertaken colonization in the name of a generalized humanity. As such, there is no intrinsic exclusion, a person can potentially attain anything they want, but this attainment will be viewed as acceding to whiteness, revalorizing its status as the arbiter of worthiness. Even the apparent counterstories of Black empires and attainments rely on the same narrative structures of history to attain their meaning and recognition.

Invention for Fanon thus entails forgetting the relationship between sovereignty and enslavement. Sovereignty is not the cure for enslavement, and enslavement is not the absence of sovereignty. Neither overcomes or succumbs to the other. While both are not erased, they are each tethered to processes of movement that can neither claim nor understand. Subject to a haunted narcissism and unable to look at itself within its own self-constituted terms, the mirror image appears only through its own disappearance. As Marriott (2011, 63) on Fanon indicates, "the black binds itself narcissistically to an irreal other, which precedes the fiction that is the condition of possibility of the black as subject."

Coming into subjectivity repeats the experience of slavery as it reiterates the consent to be a single being that is denied actualization through chaining Black people to a collective undifferentiated homogeneity that can only recognize individuation as white. Living as Black, and the regulation and self-policing this entails, requires the proficiency of mimetic capacity in order for the Black body to survive. Here the need to act correctly, quietly, without anger, to absorb all the slights and suffering without apparent complaint, have become the predominant locus and validation of self-capacity. Caught in a time that either comes too early or too late, something is always expected of the Black, where their compliance is involuntary and resistance often wasted, misdirected, or turned inward. Whatever one does, it is never good enough to change the fundamental terms of the game. At the same time, whatever constitutes creative tropes of resistance can be easily incorporated as signs of the system's capacity for reform.

So it is not that the wretched forget history; they remain in the face of it. But what is forgotten is the need to take it as anything other than an *exception*, that its organizing force was indeed exceptional, given the disjuncture between what it announced and promised and the arbitrary manifestations of violence that ensured its continuity. For the efficacy of narration, the codes through which everyday life was to be represented and deliberated depended on the arbitrary and wanton. As such, the capacity of the wretched to write themselves into the interstices, warding off violence through intricate maneuvers of hit and run incursions and warding off history through obviating the need to be represented and recognized, open up a space where ways of being can be invented. This is not as a breakthrough, not, as Fanon often wished, a complete dominance of the white other, but as the suturing of a surrounds, a place of inhabitation on the move, not necessarily stateless or even statelite, but an active display of the generativity of forgetfulness. It is a place that builds up its own evidence over time, not settling too quickly into any one dispensation, practicing the ways in which the wretched might circulate through each other, discover, and touch the differentiated sensibilities of new ventures. These ventures will inevitably be tinged by common traumas and victimhood, but that is not the only thing that they might have in common; that is not the commons that will be built on to live in this world in a different way.

FUNGIBILITY

If Fanon envisions a maneuver without precedent and without a consensually affirmed common vernacular, Tiffany Lethabo King (2016, 2019) identifies an integral fungibility at the heart of living Black that both accompanies and goes beyond the functioning of the Black body as an instrument of labor, derivation, commodification, and insurance. If Black bodies were being made into ambiguous flesh to be shaped and deployed in various fashions, at the same time, blackness was space in the making. This was not simply because in the colonization of the Americas, Black bodies were on the front lines of interfaces with the environments to be settled. It wasn't simply because they worked the fields, cleared the forests and swamps, and were sent ahead as scouts to confront hostile forces. Rather, the alignment of their efforts and labor, the ways in which they had to continuously reposition themselves in the face of carceral conditions in order to know or love each other, in order to cushion the impacts of command, were always elongating and providing textures to spaces that remained unmapped, unidentified. Multiple recesses, vacuums, and dead zones, where things took place out of view or narration, continuously occupied the heart of settlements and plantations.

According to Hortense Spillers (1987), fungibility points to such territories of cultural and political maneuver, places of secret literacies and skills, places where the unintelligibility of heterogeneous languages and practices found mechanisms of translation. As King (2016, 1028) points out, "Black figures become symbols, metaphors, and tropes of space before they are interpolated as laborers on the land." Sometimes merging with vegetation, establishing channels of communication with other creatures and spirits, assembling in ways that structured access and visibility by external witnesses, curating collective performances that were living archives of theoretical reflection and strategic instruction, fungibility was the imperative to stretch the limits of the flesh as much as possible in reverse gear from all the stretching imposed by the master's tools.

Black bodies were exposed to the surrounds, where the ontological priority was to be exposed, to distribute sense and capacity as widely as possible across the milieu of other bodies, forests, creeks, creatures, and spirits so that each would recognize each other, deflecting the ramifications of the whip, the hard labor, the broken families, and instillation of daily traumas. Again, we have a reiteration of the surrounds not only in terms of liminal precincts surrounding the plantation but also as that intricate suturing of bodily comportment, movement, exposure, stance, and signage into a collective choreography producing spaces of unsettled invention in *this* world.

MALPRACTICE

If King identifies an integral fungibility at the heart of living Black, J. Kameron Carter (2019) views such practice as an outcome of what he calls Black "malpractice." Here, the traditional regimens of the curative and restorative are both intentionally pursued and subverted. Instead of rolling out the established diagnostic terms and the normative procedures of medicine, any what he calls "god" terms are refused, that is, any terms that impose a territory on the earth. For only malpractice can recognize an earth fundamentally separate from the formats imposed to apprehend and settle it.

For Carter, malpractice seeks to rediscover a sense of otherworldliness, where inner experience is not the neurotic pursuit of finding the right representation, of developing a subject to be recognized and validated according to a hierarchy of needs or values. Rather, it is a time of the festive, something out-of-time, a time-out, or an out-time that does not correspond to any trajectory of development, realization, proficiency, or fulfillment. Malpractice is a sociality not reducible to contractual form (Moten 2018). It is something that operates outside of political settlements that apportion rights and responsibilities.

Black people have long struggled for rights, for inclusion—as they should—says Carter. But what Black experience brings to the inside of inclusion, to the articulation of rights, is not validation but a sense of errancy in all cosmologies of settlement. Black experience brings a sense of the sacred that does not put its faith in the resurrection, where things are made whole again. Rather, what is important is a dispersed and distributed crowdedness of things with its accompanying disorderly conduct that radiates outward in vectors of contagion that upend demarcations and cadastrals. It is a world of what Carter (2019, 91, 92) calls, "transshipped gods," "exilic divinities on the run," an upturning of things in their respective places. Within such a sense of upturning, things move around, stumble, and touch each other in unprecedented ways.

Carter finds a repertoire of resources for what already exists within the domains of Black worship, irreverence, exaggeration, swagger, and incantation as tools with which to continue to relate to the historical unfolding of political dispensations but without abandoning the capacity to travel on. For no people have had the experience of moving their gods and spirits across such difficult and disorderly terrain; no people were so disallowed to become set in their ways; no people were set off from so many places to unknown destinations or set off and provoked to constantly show their cards, reveal their natures. From eugenics to population sciences to public health, medicalized tropes are paraded out to patrol the health of blackness. While racism is a sickness that engenders sickness, there are manifestations of that supposed sickness that veil entire archives of practices that remain fundamentally incomplete.

Here, sickness equates to incompleteness, not wounds that can never heal, but wounds that were never simply wounds but rather a bursting forth of propositions with nowhere and everywhere to go, a body that remained incomplete, without its own time or space, as Spillers (1987) puts it, but that nevertheless remained a body after everything was said, done, and forgotten.

SET SETAL (BE CLEAN)

Moving from these America-centric resources, I want to consider a particular manifestation of an Afrofuturism that has captivated the imaginations of many African artists, musicians, and critical thinkers. The profusion of sounds, images, and words associated with Afrofuturism engage the burgeoning capacity of new generations of youths to appropriate the discourses and technologies of advanced modernity to produce their own visions and realizations of new modes of inhabiting an interplanetary system whose traces are thoroughly embedded wherever they may find themselves. From innovative uses of available technologies to the conversion of the simplest assemblage of materials into advanced machines of computation, Afrofuturism reiterates recognition of the primacy of circuits of navigation, of incessant mobility and conversion, that long characterized African populations. The systematic territorialization of African life within the rubrics of ethnicity and religion aborted a fundamental sensibility and practice whereby Africans inhabited the earth in general (Mbembe 2019) and, as such, extraplanetary travel and identification was but a next logical step.

In a much more prosaic version, I want to point to the now protracted history of *Set Setal* in Dakar as a manifestation of a forgetting being forgotten and anchored in an Afrofuturist sensibility. Originally appearing during a tumultuous period in Senegalese politics in 1990, *Set Setal* (clean and be clean, in Wolof) emerged from both the long-dilapidated working poor neighborhoods of the urban core, such as Medina, and the explosively expanding suburbs, Pikine and Guediawaye. It was a youth movement aimed at physically cleaning up their neighborhoods and thus directly rectifying their growing marginalization as both political and moral citizens. While murals were painted on seemingly every available wall and a profusion of cultural expressiveness ensued, this was more than a beautification project. Rather, it was a concerted effort to create a viable atmosphere for a repurification of collective life, a demonstration of worthiness exhibited through the capacity to work with the materials most available to them, that is, trash. Assuming the responsibility to handle the waste generated by inhabiting the city became a claim of intimacy, intimacy as the most accessible mode of eligibility for political rights (Fredericks 2014).

As a movement dedicated to "be clean," *Set Setal* was rife with ambivalence, torn between the invention of new tropes of collectivity and the reimposition of long-standing and intensely gendered notions of correct behavior, a simultaneous dependence and intolerance in a heterogeneity of expression (Diouf 1996, 2003). It also exemplified tendencies to place inordinate faith in the purported purity of religious authorities as a compulsory model for state leadership and made a constant mockery of the elite of any kind. The boundaries between *Set* as an intensely concrete, localized practice of neighborhood self-management and *Set* as an aesthetic stylization, a cultural movement, and a platform for the renewed credibility of intellectuals were always volatile and uncertain (Lambert 2016). Through government cooptation, *Set* would disrupt the work of long-standing trash workers' unions that had become a potent political force in their own right since they, too, were able to mobilize the intimate social relations attainable through waste work (Fredericks 2018).

What *Set* was able to do, beyond providing a viable locus for youths to exert a profound impact on national political contestation, was to amplify the capacity of youths to engender a renewed sense of collective life in its most practical dimensions from what was accumulating right in front them as a result of the enactment of their lives together. It thus deterred any hesitations about why they might be gathered in the streets in such large numbers, as such gatherings were used as occasions to mark and imagine their environments in a different way. "One wall led to yet another," a common saying had it. Youths went so far as to even extract "taxation" from public vehicles crossing their territories in order to fund their projects. Still, *Set* was a movement replete with its own multiple contradictions. Its inability to reconcile immunization against the dirt of politics with exposure to the impure relationalities of discovery across different neighborhoods and forms of expression later became conundrums to be expressed through the proliferation of hip-hop and urban guerilla poetry across Dakar.

While *Set Setal* as a discernible movement has waxed and waned over the years, it has endured in various forms, most recently as a practice of dissimulation and intervention that calls attention to an array of urban problems and, most particularly, to exorbitant spending on infrastructural and artistic projects of questionable viability. Buildings and intersections are occupied to visualize alternative uses; automobile traffic is navigated not simply in the pursuit of commercial activities during go-slows but to advance public education campaigns on issues of migration and unemployment. *Set* is infused as an incentive in multiple social media platforms, when a flood of images and messages is produced documenting both instances of incivility and uncleanliness across the public sphere, as well as in all the small initiatives that take place on a daily basis to ameliorate insalubrious conditions.

Set is able to forget about its past manifestations and contradictions, forget about it being forgotten as the very basis through which the current national administration administers a new cleaning campaign as part of its policy of emergence—that is, its policy emphasizing the need for a new Senegalese mentality and civility in order for its real potentials to emerge. *Set* continues to try to take back from official state discourse the tropes of collective empowerment that belong instead to the people; it remains indifferent to the ways in which it is inevitably coopted into a homogenizing sense of urban responsibility, where cleanliness is incumbent on each and every individual. Yet, it replays its refrain in new ways, constantly demonstrating a capacity to show up in new conditions with new tools, unencumbered by particular terrestrial histories, defying genre and time. Proffering a kind of generic purity, *Set* may be a ruse, a way that generations of youths repeatedly and playfully return to the "crime" with new forensic evidence, forgetting any solutions, past or future.

EXPOSURE

The residents of Jakarta are known for their cynicism. Everyday transactions are replete with a turn of phrase or physical gesture that not so much undermines the original intention of that to which it was a response, as enforces a suspension of judgment, instantiates a moment of uncertainty where the subsequent unfolding of events might go in very different directions. A constant series of metacommentaries accompanies all kinds of exchange with wordplay and mixed-up genres. Teachers handing out exam papers become the unemployed hawking flyers for yard sales; checkout queues at cash registers become waiting lines for electoral voting; women's prayer recitals use Quranic verses as codes to evaluate the sexual capacities of neighborhood men. Constantly self-effacing, enduring the city requires never taking oneself or anyone else seriously, if only to supplement everyday transactions with small surfeits of negotiability.

A pervasive cynicism is particularly manifested in the popular social media responses to each and every governmental decree, when tens of thousands of postings all try to outdo each other in the inventiveness of their disdain and mockery. This is particularly the case when new programmatic initiatives and policies are couched in terms of the fundamental values to which Indonesians would normatively subscribe. Every mention of democracy, freedom, national pride, or religious authenticity is met with an onslaught of comedic derision and hyperbole. To a certain extent, such practice represents the afterlife of the rollicking, irreverent, and rough-cut style of Jakartan urban life that characterized its largely working-poor neighborhoods in the period prior to the ascendancy of middle-class values with their emphasis on "doing the right thing." The latter consisted of disciplined, incremental attainments through the cultivation of proper behavior, converting the self through the propriety of property, treating the self as something worthy of investment. For many of those who came to consider themselves middle class, if only through expanded consumption, there is an increased preoccupation with questions about what that consumption has really enabled, and the sense that relinquishing the repertoires of street-level wheeling and dealing has left them trapped in dead-end jobs and lifestyles.

While not mapping precisely onto Foucault's (2011) late lectures on cynicism as a rejection of the manifestations of what a person claims to accept as principle, as a scandalous rendering of operative presuppositions, these reflections of Jakartan cynicism do locate the possibilities of accessing a different kind of world from a break with the "settled" forms of existence. These cynical postures implicitly indicate a forgetting of the conventions and connotations that otherwise bring order to everyday life, yet at the same time, they also convey an injunction about forgetting that they have indeed been forgotten. Thus, those very same conventions persist, with all the grammars of decorum, social acceptability, deference, and acquiescence. They continue to do their work of cultivating a specific atmosphere and set of procedures through which individuals and groups are brought together. Yet they also owe their existence to their very availability to be converted into something else, as they function as the very "raw materials" of such conversions and ironic twists and turns.

Perhaps more salient to Foucault's intent in his thirteenth lecture of *The Courage of Truth*, his conception of a life that is other comes through the ways in which increasing numbers of Jakartans expose their lives to a more comprehensive forgetting of familiar conditions and procedures of settlement. During the past several years, I have been following the itineraries of scores of individuals and households who have vacated the urban core neighborhoods (where I worked) for more provisional destinations across the peripheries of Jakarta's expansive urban region. Suspending any pretense of pursuing long-range plans, their search is for dispositions that are adequate *for now*, already anticipating the possibility that whatever is viable in the present might be short-lived, requiring at least the feeling of having moved on, even if remaining in a particular place and occupation. While some of these households were priced out of their original homes or forced out by the incursions of well-resourced developments, most volitionally pursued an exit,

97

not because they did not value the considerable achievements that they and their localities had made over the years in constructing livelihoods and territories that worked well in so many ways. Rather, they had concluded that continued attachments to these ways of life impeded their ability to come to terms with where the city was headed and what kinds of behaviors and decisions would be required of them in order to deal with the futures to come. It wasn't that they knew precisely what was required of them or had a precise image of the changes underway, but rather that the situation required being exposed to a larger "background" of events and processes, to something "out there," which meant that it was not advantageous to put too much effort or too many resources into resettling, concretizing a definitive destination or livelihood. It was more important to maintain a capacity to circulate, to explore what is "out there" in a wider, diffuse sense, rather than to consolidate a life within a specific place. Of course, the pragmatics of needing an address, of being able to park one's belongings and particular family members meant the acquisition of some affordable place of stability from which other household members could venture across multiple short-term accommodations, jobs, and other opportunities—a process partially sustained through the continuous re-suturing of temporary social networks largely made up of those who were neither friends nor strangers.

Those who undertake new lives in the periphery are exposed to situations where there may be little in terms of institutional support or urban services. There is the exposure that comes with concluding that one's familiar ways of managing daily affairs are insufficient, and that the present composition of family and friends may not be enough to keep up with things. Here is the exposure to new circumstances over which one cannot exert much control. The itineraries of those residents trying to engage new opportunities, new incomes, and new places of everyday operation result in their exposure to multiple contestations, power dynamics, and forms of authority with which they have only limited understanding or ways of dealing. All around are those prepared to take advantage of their vulnerabilities, their desire for some sense of direction. But they also see others around them take inordinate risks to do something different with their lives, and sometimes they also see the evidence that these risks indeed work. Here, exposure means being attuned to events and circumstances beyond one's normal routines and interests. So exposure is a multifaceted intersection of vulnerability and opportunity; it is a byproduct of precarity but also a way of dealing with that precarity at the same time, and this doubleness of sense is embodied by the notion of the background or the "out there" that is repeatedly referred to.

Within this politics of nascent inhabitation, it is important to remain exposed to the multiplicity of elements, to hedge one's bets so that it is possible to concretely navigate uncertain terrain. The message is: don't act too quickly, don't make too many commitments, and try to pay attention to all the different events happening around you. Then you will understand where you are.

What I construe from all these invocations of the background, then, is an alternating reference to something "out there" that remains to be crystalized as a specific image, event, or infrastructure. But it is also something intimate, within one's own capacities to put together. As one of my associates, Didi, puts it, "Jakarta is still trying to put together the big story about itself.... You can't really read what it is yet, but you see it being put together out there; it may not ever happen because, you see, Jakarta doesn't really have one place anymore.... So it's up to you to give it one."

The background is also an affordance. By virtue of attending or being exposed to that which goes beyond the immediate scenes in front of you, or to the images of a discernible horizon, the observer is granted a view of the city that is able to bring places, actors, and events together that are otherwise left apart. So in its basic sense, the background combines a willingness to suspend the judgment that what you see is what things are, an acknowledgment that beyond the immediacy of a person's context, there is a field of vision that can be grasped and composed in excess of what is presented, and a belief that this willingness to see in a different way, a way that does not tie everything together into a coherent image, will enable one to better navigate the ins and outs of everyday urban life. Less a matter of actively creating specific conditions, the background refers to the importance of being exposed, even if being exposed leaves one vulnerable to unexpected or even undesirable changes. But this is the risk that residents often intend to take. As another associate, Fadli, remarks: "I think that in all of my train rides across Jakarta, all of the things I have to do and all of the things that I just end up doing for little reason at all, that I am being exposed to something I can't quite talk about clearly, but I know it will change my life, and this is what I want.... It's not because what I have gone through has been so hard; no, I have forgotten about all of that; I don't care if anyone wasn't paying attention; what I want is besides all of that."

THREE

REBELLION
WITHOUT
REDEMPTION

Spirit sees, language sees, the body visits.
It always exceeds its site, by displacement.
The subject sees, the body visits, surpasses
its own position, goes out from its role or word.
. . . The body goes out from the body in all
senses (*dans tous les sens*), the sensible knots
up this knot, the sensible in which the body
never persists in the same plane or content
but plunges and lives in a perpetual exchange,
turbulence, whirlwind, circumstance.
—Michel Serres, *The Five Senses*

In chapter 2 I proposed some features of experiences between forgetting and memory within spaces where distinctions between the collapsed and the generative become matters of strategic decision, of alternations between running ahead and staying behind, of passionate engagement and calculated indifference. The rhythms of remembering to forget and forgetting to remember open up distinct horizons of perspective and action, while neither maneuver can replace or undo the other. Time is a matter of *accompaniment*, of never being alone within a singular present, of each place and moment being inhabited by lures and haunting. What accompanies is not guarantor, investor, or judge. Rather it is a stubborn reminder of incompletion, that something more remains to be done.

As such, this is a strange accompaniment. It is neither like the professions of a lover that makes us feel complete, nor like that of a savior capable of making us whole again. Accompaniment is itself a kind of hole, both in the sense of gnawing unease and something to crawl through. In this chapter, I want to posit this accompaniment as an ongoing rebelliousness, a form of companionship that continuously throws us off the familiar stride or cherished aspiration. It is an accompaniment that doesn't settle into our households, but instead pushes and turns us across different directions; it is an enduring relationship in flight. It is a flight toward something intensely specific; it is not a becoming anything whatsoever. It brings to this world a sense of *thisness* that does not claim to be unique or unprecedented, but just *this* enunciation, gift, or proposition, in *this* time and in *this* world.

At the End of the Day, What Do We Have?

In the vastness of the urban hinterlands, both seemingly depleted and spectacularly filled spaces simultaneously succumb to and resist the gravitational pulls registered by dominant imaginaries of the good life, the effective or transcendent life. All the imaginaries that the city sought to materialize have their inevitable dark sides and dependence on cheap labor and life (Brickell 2014; Das and Randeria 2015; Doshi and Raganathan 2017). From tenement towns and suburban barrios to *jardins extensios*, urban regions are now largely made up of built environments that look and feel like a kind of endless surrounds, places to settle sleep and a few domestic functions. These are places full of interiors without definition, sales made and often withdrawn before any building is completed, or where buildings fall apart long before they can be paid off (Samson 2015; Coelho, Mahadevia, and Williams 2020). It may appear that these surrounds are the mere warehouses for a long unruly urban majority and the manifestations of a distributed system of residing, storing, fabricating, processing, extracting, and speculating that can take place out of view, without having to consider and act on the political articulations among critical urban functions and populations. Yet, the itineraries of movement and circulation that sometimes transpire among these distributions forge collectivities in motion that continuously rehearse different engagements that surrounds these surrounds as a kind of unanticipated accompaniment.

In the past several years I have witnessed how urban peripheries that grow more and more distant from the historic urban core are ridden with crisscrossing tracks of only provisionally settled projects. Whether because of forced evictions, voluntary displacement, desperate speculations, or well-worked-out calculations about affordability and future prospects, these peripheries come to hold wide ranging vulnerabilities and energetic initiatives. But instead of these reflecting determined efforts to settle matters in place, to dig in and plan a viable life, most convey a sense of temporariness. There is the need of having somewhere to put belongings, to park aging relatives, or to organize an official address. Otherwise, many of those who reside there seem to be in constant motion, keeping costs down so that what resources are available can be staked on more opportunistic ventures across wider swathes of the urban region, where more lucrative or personally compatible opportunities might be found. Increasingly, everyday life is lived through multiple itineraries of shifting household members around, accessing goods and services piecemeal in various arrangements, and circulating through part-time jobs.

In an urban life characterized by intensifying dispossession and consumption, what are urban majorities—the poor, working- and lower-middle-classes—left with? What do they, in the end, really have—not in the sense of property or assets—not what they can lay claim to, but more what remains with them, in their midst, that which can be used now but which does not entail a debt that can never be paid off? My friends Momen Al Husseiny and Caroline Kihato would argue that what such residents have is the *maybe*— that things maybe go one way or another in a moment that is singularly yours and yours alone, a moment when everything that has taken place so far does not generate the odds of a particular probability.

All the traumas of the past, everything that has been tried so far, whether it works or not, all the times one has fallen down and picked oneself up again do not prepare you for what will take place now. All that suffering that won't be redeemed but that has thickened your skin, turned the surface of your body into a confusing map of contradictory itineraries; all this comes both to matter and to not matter. Whether you pass through the roadblock, manage to mobilize a life's savings into something tangible, or manage to turn that corner just before the police or debt collectors arrive, this time of the maybe, more than simply a wager or speculation, is a continuous rebellion against what is on offer, against how one is regarded. But it is a rebellion without redemption.

102

All that suffering and labor, all those struggles, Lord, perhaps in the end do produce a definitive destination that makes it all worth it. If you have managed to break through to some other side, it is as if the accomplishment is yours and yours alone. But the sense of the *maybe*—maybe I make it or maybe I don't—is not up to you, is not a reflection of your skill or worthiness. Rather, what you possess, at the end of the day, is an accompaniment. Something else is there besides you, something you possess that possesses you. It is a situation where you are tethered to a mind of its own that is also yours. Your possessions, in the end, are the possibilities of being possessed in a rebellion against whatever you think you are at that moment when a line in the sand, or on a road or screen, is drawn.

For when you appear at that roadblock, at that crossroads, it is not your history, your eligibility, your skill that will see you through (Nancy 2016). Everything you present at that moment may count for nothing in a decision that is completely arbitrary and for which you will have no grounds for appeal. At the same time, all the times when you might be deemed ineligible to show up at that roadblock, that courthouse, that convocation, where those who judge claim that you are just not good enough, just not sufficiently prepared, also in the end don't matter. You don't give them any mind, and that, too, is part of the *maybe*. It is a situation where no matter what you have doesn't count, and where all that you don't have is also refused count. On the one hand, you can be dismissed for no reason; on the other, dismissal is not a reason for anything; you will carry on no matter what. Each trajectory accompanies the other; each is a matter of mutual possession. That which is present, accounted for, presented and performed, is dismissed, just as the grounds for dismissal are irrelevant in an adamant claim for endurance. This, then, is what residents are left with; this is what they have.

On the Accompaniment of *Djinn* (the Time of Women)

In recent decades, much has been said about the kind of ways the "human" should or should not be retained as a concept. What is the human's culpability as a species or political entity in the possible extinction of its own ongoingness? How has the "human" been used to reduce large swathes of human life to the status of the inhuman? Without entering into these debates per se, my intent is simply to raise the question of accompaniment to whatever journey the "human" has made. Not dissimilar to Donna Haraway's (2003) notion of companion species, what kind of companions might we have? Here, I want to dig into the traditions of popular Islamic histories to pose the possibilities of *djinn* as one way of thinking about the surrounds; djinn as companions who are never one thing but always a shape-shifting concrescence of different forces and images that concretize a specific dilemma or possibility. A roadblock, a courthouse, a city hall.

Djinns may be identified with particular names or features in an act of figuring that simultaneously brings together tensions in a living enactment, while embodying the reality that any agency is a *composite* agency, all the way down. Whatever individual decisiveness, integrity, or self-conscious reflection we may possess is accompanied by and exposed to a technological mode of existence, which is what djinn basically is. Based on the single element of fire, that which was stolen from the Gods, djinn is technical, in its capacity to convert, remake, transmute, and transform without any overarching objective or political purpose. Its operations are not guaranteed by any essential harmonization. Always shaped by a gap of synchronization, djinn is incessant sociopolitical antagonism, the possibility of rebellion without end. It is this possibility of rebellion, of upending any definition of purpose or redemption that is the accompaniment of the human (Amadu 1972).

Morehshin Allahyari (2019) is an Iranian American artist who has attempted to recuperate the voluminous stories of djinn across different Islamic cultures in what she calls "a time of women." She produces 3D printed female djinn figures in a project titled "She Who Sees the Unknown." These refigurings, drawn from the various ways in which female djinn are cited in the Quran, seek specifically to embody a "time of women" at work in contemporary renditions of colonialism, climate change, and racial and gender injustice. Djinn as a locus of hybridization is deployed to exert specific forces of life. I am interested in djinn not so much as a distinct kind of entity as an entitling of force that compels a particular way of paying attention to the world, of responding to calls potentially issued by everything and everywhere.

Across various performances, Allahyari has presented four djinn in particular:

HUMA, with its three heads, two facing opposite directions, and a third facing upward into a future, with legs splayed, is the transmission of heat for those who have been left behind, a medium through which their forgotten presence makes itself felt. Here is where technology becomes an instrument of justice, and where what is institutionalized as well-being becomes a desert, to be deserted. If there is to be any redemption, there can be only redemption for all. There is no eligibility, no hierarchy or property.

AISHA QUANDISHA is she who can crack, open up, unlock, or render vulnerable that which is most secure, identify the holes in any policy or dictate. In such dehiscence there can be no re-suturing, no new skin to cover the wound; the only way to survive is to participate in the exposure that is availed, to live outside the terms through which one has recognized oneself as complete or integral.

YA'OOJ MAJOOJ has traditionally been figured as the instigator of chaos. With its multiple heads protruding from a reptile body, she is the purveyor of *fitna*, which underlines the definition of every social body. She is the precipitant of sovereignty, that elemental distinguishing of friend and enemy, compelling walls to be built, but within which her face cannot be held. For, she insists upon accompanying every social order and is that which any polity cannot do without.

THE LAUGHING SNAKE, Allahyari's final figure, is a female serpent who winds her way haphazardly across every city in any direction, devouring all she confronts. The only way to stop her is for men to hold a mirror in front of her. Encountering her image, she literally, after many days, dies laughing. Rather than being alarmed, enchanted, or alienated by her representation, the serpent simply convulses with the hilarity that somehow representation could be at all adequate to the reality at hand. How she is understood is so wildly incongruous with her own conception of herself, that she finds the situation nearly impossible to grasp. How stupid are men to think that somehow institutionalizing a confrontation with the image could be capable of doing anything? For this is an act paradoxically effective only because the excessive hilarity it provokes makes the serpent forget that she needs to eat.

Each of these djinn, then, is neither a curse nor a prophecy, nor a willing coconspirator to human desires to inflict harm. Neither are djinns cures. As the Quran makes clear, djinns are capable of both obedience and disobedience to divine will. They are rather technical operations, openers, heat inducers, shape-shifters, navigational instruments, disrupters, and thresholds potentially used for radically different purposes, all of which are unable to contain them. For Muslim popular cultures, they extend the time of women from that of caring, reproducing, seducing, dissimulating, birthing, and gossiping to fundamentally *industrial* actions responsible for ensuring the possibilities of endurance where there otherwise may seem to be none.

In chapter 2, I talked about past engagements with Bloods gangs in Kinshasa. In one brief anecdote, I cited how "51," a Bloods gang member who claimed to oversee an international tribunal, talked about the immanence of a "time of women" that was coming in the possible evacuation of the city, an evacuation that would be forgotten so that the same conditions might be reinhabited in different ways and the the urban core might be approached as an urban surrounds. In Jean-Pierre Bekolo's 2005 film *Les Saignantes* (The Bloodettes), this "time of women" is demonstrated by the way in which the main characters, Majolie and her friend Chouchou, must overturn the political power structure in order simply to live as they are, two youths, who perhaps have an entire life ahead of them.

Like many young women in their circumstances, Cameroon in 2024, when the film's story takes place, does not look any different from Cameroon at the time the film was made. Both women attempt to gain access to economic possibilities through sexual encounters with the elite. They not only make their bodies available to be used by men but enact the sexual with such extraordinary choreographies as to make it inevitable that the men will submit to their subsequent requests, reiterating the age-old stereotype of women as the real sexual predators. At the film's opening, however, the head of security that Majolie has fucked suddenly dies, forcing her to quickly come up with a plan for disposing of the body. She turns to her friend Chouchou for help and, implicitly, to Chouchou's mother, the woman closest to her who knows the rites of the djinn *Mevungu*, who must inevitably accompany the young women on this mission to save themselves.

In Beti culture, Mevungu embodies the empowerment of women necessary to combat forces that cause misfortune, such as failed harvests or unexplained death. It entails nocturnal gatherings where women spend the night singing, dancing, eating, and celebrating the clitoris of Mevungu, which is said to be more powerful than any phallus. In Bekolo's film, Mevungu becomes a mobile embodiment of multiple pasts that could have been, a thoroughly technological force, neither intrinsically virtuous nor destructive. It is neither living nor nonliving, but rather an intersection of countervailing forces that could go in many different directions—that is, the source of rebellion against any hegemonic narrative, that which gathers up all the residues of interactions that are constrained and shaped by specific political orders and offers different arrangements and dispositions.

At first, acting from their perceived vulnerability, the young women dispose of the victim's body with a local butcher, placing wads of cash in his hand. The butcher takes everything but the head. Soon the women recall, however, that the most important occasion, particularly in terms of political elevation, is that of "wakes for important people," where the political class gathers to perform exaggerated acts of mourning and quickly figure out ways to reposition themselves around the nascent absence. Additionally, in a city where sexual violence is always to be expected, throwing oneself over the casketed body of the deceased is one relatively safe place for prostate women not to be threatened with rape. Having snuck into one of the wakes in order to drink and eat for free, and having spent their available money on taxis and butchers, Majolie decides that she and Chouchou should stage a wake for the chief of security who had passed away during her extraordinary sexual acrobatics. But for this, they will need to find a body to accompany the head, and much of the film centers on this quest and their unfolding relationship with the minister of state forced upon them in this project.

The film ends with the women seducing, fighting, and killing the minister of state in order to save one of their friends from being raped. During the entire film, even the investigations conducted by the noncorrupt police are rendered completely useless. Bekolo, indeed, intersperses the narrative with cuts where he posts questions, such as: What does it mean to tell a detective story in a country where everything is denied? Even as the djinn, Mevungu, provides the surfeit of force necessary to destroy the minister of state, his dead body is full of potentially lethal toxins, of which the young women must remove all traces in order to survive. The film, having taken place entirely at night, closes during daylight as Majolie and Chouchou are seen happily wandering among the populous in a local market, living an ordinary life deemed otherwise impossible without their protracted rebellion. Here the very possibility of two young women accompanying each other is predicated on the surrounds of a well-known companion, Mevungu, whose character, disposition, and potentiality in the present cannot be known in detail based on that familiarity alone. As such, this is not a force that can be controlled. It can be called upon, but with complete uncertainty as to how things are going to turn out; there is simply no way of knowing. For rebellion cannot show the same old cards; it cannot give itself away in advance. It is, again, a time of the *maybe*.

Material Resistance

At other times, rebellion and accompaniment are rendered more tacit within the daily operations of collective life. Rebellion can be inscribed into the very materiality of how people live together. Rumah Susun Tanah Tinggi is a large social housing development in Jakarta, built twenty-two years ago, which now accommodates some four thousand residents in eight four-story concrete structures, with each unit measuring between 35 and 50 square meters. Over

3.1 | Rumah Susun Tanga Tinggi,
Jakarta. Photograph by Ifardianto.

the years, residents have sometimes extended and enclosed balconies, redesigned the external facades of their interior entries, constructed elaborate
pulley systems and external bamboo frames to increase the space available
for laundry and to transfer small items across apartment units. The ground
floor entrances have been extended by a constantly redesigned network of
sheds, lean-tos, and canopies for small commercial activities and meeting
places. The unusually voluminous hallways that traverse the complex are
replete with not only various stored items but the compositions of various
projects, from birdcages, herbal medicines, card games, maker spaces with
their collection of discarded equipment, photoshopped backgrounds for
Tik-Tok videos churned out by young kids, small looms for weaving, tape
recorders, ducks, and improvised kitchens for culinary snack production, all
in violation of the rules.

Passageways accommodate not only bodily traffic but also propositions
about spatial possibilities, about what can be done, without an effort to consolidate space or institutionalize a niche as discrepant things and activities seem
to work their way through and around each other. Material arrangements thus

108

become propositions. Instead of demanding right-of-way for unimpeded access from one's domicile to the larger external world, the daily challenge is what can be done with traffic, with the incessantly strange assortment of propositions that refuse consensus. Such propositions do not so much demand to be acknowledged as slip into still other propositions and temporary assemblages. Far from being a preference for chaos, these propositions, this intermingling of things and their proponents, is a lure for residents to reconsider their orientations to their present conditions. It is a renewal of the affective atmosphere of a housing complex clearly heaving its way through attempts to accommodate its sheer numbers, from the elders with limited mobility to the young unable to stay put.

The critical element of this construction is that any resident's "project" should resonate with multiple lines of connection, that each project and proposition should neither provoke excessive antagonism or feelings of vulnerability nor extract space for its own profit. Such had been a matter of concern in the now torn-down shacks inserted into back alleyways that were often used for drug sales. Tensions inevitably exist between the residents' reasonable desire to carve out as much of a normal life as they can and the recognition that Tanah Tinggi has long capitalized on its reputation as the "black heart" of Jakarta. The neighborhood is full of unruly, undomesticated characters plying licit and illicit trades in ways that make the difference between them indiscernible. The tension inherent in the desire to do the "right thing" according to the ascendent middle-class inflected norms of Islam and the widespread recognition that the "right thing" is only going to take you so far constantly plays out as the back-and-forth drama of the complex. Still, this is a district rooted in the generativity of the *maybe*, where residents believe that the intensive mixtures of functional and dysfunctional materials, brazen commentary and outrageous claims, and work deployed playfully across long hours will bring to life something unanticipated and transformative.

For such an eventuality to work, nothing can be imposed for sure. Rumah Susun Tanah Tinggi has indeed been the site of many attempted impositions. Competing drug gangs, political parties, religious groupings, brokers, commercial bosses, and hungry bureaucrats always try to imprint their agendas on the place through cajoling, luring, promising, providing, or forcefully imposing their will, sowing distrust, and forging complicities. While such agendas may sometimes win the day, over the years none has succeeded for long, and impositions don't set in for protracted periods of time. Not with the webs of intensely local and changing propositions materialized through the interconnections of space, along hallways, yards,

109

rooftops, entryways, parking lots, and other common spaces. Not with their growing array of objects circulating across disparate endeavors, as well as the intercalated choreographies of cooking, washing, cleaning, repairing, praying, joking, arguing, and so forth, all with their own tapestries of affective registers. There is what Laura Kemmer (2020) has called a domain of *material resistance* that goes beyond the familiar tropes of political agency. Resistance is in the very arrangement of materials in space, the propositions that ensue from these arrangements of what could be done. Resistance entails the ways in which these propositions are incorporated into others and mapped onto the shifting social interdependencies of residents who refuse to be "resettled" into dispositions that promise either betterment, rectification, or redemption.

Such resistance maintains the possibility of eventuality, of the *maybe*, where the ongoing intersection of different approaches to and outcomes from common residence might proceed to generate experiences that are easily codified or structured by those of the past and that engender new collective capacities of endurance. Material resistance indicates a surfeit of affective charge in residents' relationships with their immediate environment and generates a surrounds as the Rumah Susun is literally surrounded with the incipient propositions that emerge through their various efforts to curate the different spaces across the complex. Like all manifestations of resistance, there is nothing that is unequivocally generative or virtuous.

While the material resistance conveyed through the process of continuous rearrangement and updating may clear a path for unanticipated feelings, initiatives, and capacities, residents may also be inclined to hold on too long either in their compulsion to revise or let things be, or because of their attachment to a specific version of themselves that they come to be known for or invest in (Berlant 2011). The force of eventuality is that its dispositions remain unknown. There can be speculation, prediction, and probability. But when actions are undertaken specifically to anticipate something new coming to the fore, a certain disappointment will inevitably ensue.

Eventuality cannot adhere to the same logics as planning. There may be faith in the pursuit of particular tacit, collective processes, but whether they will produce anything useful or not, usable or not, remains a question. It is just this question that is operationalized by material resistance, that temporality where nothing, something, or everything might happen. For disappointment registers as a decay in the energies of residents and marks their susceptibility to grand narratives of conspiracies and promised salvation. Material resistance is something that requires continuous tending and curiosity, not as a receptacle for the deepest hopes of individuals, households, or community, but rather as a step aside from daily routine. It is an engagement with a shape-shifting entity—all its propositions—that spawns the complex and embodies the traces of pasts that might have led in different directions, a coresidence with djinn, a technicity of souls.

The everyday acts of proposing, materialized in small endeavors and their compositional objects, are forms of address calling upon the attentiveness of others. This call is not to say, "Hey, look at me, here I am, this is mine, this represents me," but rather has sense of "take me up, somehow, call upon me, fold me in, but at the same time, *let me be*." This mode of address seeks intimacy with an aggregation of different forces at work in the complex. This is done not with the intent of channeling to do harm or advance individual interests but to maintain an element of enchantment, uncanny wonder within the routinized mechanization of everyday rituals that are necessary to keep seven hundred households in such close proximity living on.

What Happens When Almost Nothing Is Left

The refusal of redemption is exemplified in Jean Genet's incendiary final dramatic work, *The Screens*, written just prior to the end of the Algerian War. Here the most wretched of characters, the Arabs, are surrounded by complete indifference to their existence and the opportunistic efforts to capitalize on their desperation for recognition as they are assigned the dirty jobs of effacing the scourge of French colonialism. They are surrounded by maternal invocations to completely debase themselves, amplifying the very wretchedness that they represent.

Rewritten, the play was first performed in the United States in New York in 1971, and it was staged as a series of screens situated at various levels across an expansive stage. The projections of French modernity are literally figured as projectiles against the possibilities of any self-determination, against any effort to valorize life emerging behind the screens. Political discourse of any kind remains a freak show, full of inflated claims and cartoon identities. The combatants for liberation end up parodying the very forms of entrapment they seek to overturn, seemingly indifferent to their own elevation of the inauthentic sentiments of freedom and democracy that the enemy has long ceased to believe in anyway.

The French simply want to wallow in blood and will use any civilized excuse to do so. When they go "high" there is nowhere else for the wretched to go but lower than low. For only then, in a life of continuous revolt, exhausting all the proposals for rectification on offer, will a path be cleared for the wretched to gather each other up in equanimity and mutual respect simply for what they are. The time of women in Genet is not that of uplift but a refusal to be dignified for revolutionary fervor or exhibit tenderness toward the cause.

In the following, Pierre, a French parachutist, confronts the Mother, the embodiment of that call for utter debasement, now armed:

PIERRE: [*With anxiety.*] Granny, you playing a game or something? You're too old for that. What're you doing?

THE MOTHER: [*Suddenly out of patience, she vigorously pulls the strap, pressing her knee against the soldier's back.*] I'm pulling. [*She imitates the sound of a machine gun, then spits in her hands and pulls harder.*]

PIERRE: [*With sudden panic.*] It's not possible? You haven't done that, have you, old girl?

THE MOTHER: [*She gives the corpse a kick.*] It's not true, you're not dead? Stand up. On your feet! You're not dead. I didn't kill you, did I? [*She kneels beside the corpse.*] Answer me, I beg you, answer, little soldier of France, love, my love, my pussycat, my little mousie, stand up, come on, up, you trash! [*She straightens and picks up the belt.*] He's dead all right, the swine!

Even here, any act of courage is accidental, unintended, but it doesn't matter. The real worry for the wretched in this play is that the liberators will name public squares after them, freeze them into someone else's memory. Thus, betrayal is the only way out. For Said, the closest the play comes to a main character, to be a thief is to be despised by everyone, but this is the only way to avoid becoming an object of theft. Revolutions cannot be successfully waged without thieves, without those willing to overstep the bounds, to commit acts that can be immediately condemned by all sides. Yet the thieves, the wretched, may indeed refuse to have anything to do with that which is brought about by their "good works." They betray the possibility of their own redemption, preferring to remain wild cards, potentially associated with any endeavor, which they will continue to betray and exhaust until all that is left are themselves just on the outskirts of the city, just on the outskirts of the wreckage that is their own creation, all things in disarray and to be rearranged without plan or purpose. Maybe it will work; maybe it will not.

Any person with a chance to change the course of the world must come to grips with the possibility that there is no redemption. Perhaps the only thing that can be done is to turn away from the inevitability of repetition, of the way individuals are continuously lured into thinking that behind the veil, under the floorboards, rests buried truth, buried treasure. Perhaps no writer has come as close to this possibility as Fernanda Melchor (2020) in her recent novel, *Hurricane Season*. The book is set in one of those urban hinterlands, in this case, La Matosa, some fifteen miles from the official border of Veracruz, Mexico. It is a place of passing through: truck stops, cheap bars and brothels, roadside stands, and checkpoints set amidst a landscape of largely fallow sugarcane fields, dying factories, and oil fields. The story centers on the killing of a witch, imbued with every conceivable fantasy and derogation, and who actually is trans, living in a hut in the irrigation canals. She practices traditional medicine and throws wild clandestine parties. She is constantly visited by the lovelorn, the sick, and the aspirant seeking visions and cures, even as she is vilified by all.

La Matosa is a world inhabited by the perpetually wounded. Every relation seems characterized by a nauseating mixture of desire, disgust, cruelty, and betrayal. Any act of tenderness is immediately undermined, every sexual act a medium through which the most despicable and desirable become indiscernible. Young girls slaughtered for fun by narcos end up as taco filling; grandmothers and mothers willingly abandon their children to any fate that provides a momentary meal or fuck; betrayal of loved ones becomes inseparable from any feeling of tenderness. Young men constantly humiliate each other as the only available form of solidarity, with the exception of sucking any cock that comes along willing to pay for it.

It is a world that never seems to exhaust its own wretchedness, where everyone blames everyone else for their misfortune. Melchor conveys this world with the most proficient and propulsive of run-on sentences that never seem to run out of breath and instead capture our desire that somehow in all the muck and madness there is a route out of this implosive maze. But it never comes. No matter how determined the inhabitants may be to escape, either through suicide or jobs elsewhere, they are trapped by their toxic dependencies, their inability to separate out all the conflicting emotions so that they might be decisive somehow and somewhere. They are unable to relent on the fantasy they know well not to be true, that under the witch's house there are enormous amounts of gold to be found.

But it wasn't even for this that the witch had her throat cut in a canal, but rather from an intent that is simply banal. All that seems possible from this

113

time of women betraying and bad-mouthing each other is that they faintly recognize there is something else that accompanies their perpetual cruelty:

> They say the place is hot, that it won't be long before they send in the marines to restore order in the region. They say the heat's driven the locals crazy, that it's not normal—May and not a single drop of rain—and that the hurricane season's coming hard, that it must be bad vibes, jinxes, causing all that bleakness: decapitated bodies, maimed bodies, rolled-up, bagged-up bodies dumped on the roadside or in hastily dug graves on the outskirts of town. Men killed in shootouts and car crashes and revenge killings between rival clans; rapes, suicides, "crimes of passion," as the journalists call them. Like that twelve-year-old kid who killed his girlfriend in a jealous rage on discovering that she was pregnant with his father's baby, down in San Pedro Potrillo. They say that's why the women are on edge, especially in La Matosa. They say that, come evening, they gather on their porches to smoke filterless cigarettes and cradle their youngest babes in their arms, blowing their peppery breath over those tender crowns to shoo away the mosquitos, basking in what little breeze reaches them from the river, when at last the town settles into silence and you can just about make out the music coming from the highway brothels in the distance, the rumble of the trucks as they make their way to the oilfields, the baying of dogs calling each other like wolves from one side of the plain to the other; the time of evening when the women sit around telling stories with one eye on the sky, looking out for that strange white bird that perches on the tallest trees and watches them with a look that seems to want to tell them something... there is no treasure in there, no gold or silver or diamonds or anything more than a searing pain that refuses to go away. (Melchor 2020, 194–95)

Here, a djinn appears in a most stripped-down way, as a white bird, seeming to tell the residents of La Matosa to turn away from the prospects that the witch, whom they defiled, despised, and then killed, holds out the prospect of any fortune. Whether they pay attention or not is another matter.

While this might seem an overly bleak assessment of a "time of women," Melchor implicitly points to a final indifference to time itself and all that it represents—all the incessant "rolling with the punches" and obligatory commitments to a better life that wield such a tight grip on the sentiments of those who perhaps know better. Know that life has and will remain a spasmodic grasping at straws, a perpetually low blow. As Joy James (2016, 258) unabashedly insists, the metaphysics of a good life is made possible only by a "captive maternal," by women who, through tending to all the myriad of details necessary to keep everyone fed, cleaned, educated, and nursed, maintain the edifice of an onward development. Where "the chit-chat of the little cuts and rat-like gnawing is the norm." For James, time is the endless duration of neediness. While love might suspend time, it cannot restore it—that lost time of seeing how one thing leads to another, where fruition and development are upended in the sheer repetition of compensating for trauma, covering for the absences of those incarcerated, killed, debilitated. This is a job that falls time and time again to women elders not allowed to grow old.

Even as the time of women has always also been a time of rebellion, the costs entailed do not produce unequivocal victories. As James (2018, 280) reminds us: "Entering the public realm of protest requires leaving to some extent the private realm of reproductive or domestic labor. Who will now pick up kids after school, get dinner on the table, oversee homework, and help family manage grief? Surrogate maternals, many times younger or older women, such that teenage daughters or grandmothers might be utilized to fill the void more than their masculine counterparts."

To take on the world with a militant sensibility fully cognizant of the prospective impossibilities of transformation also might draw upon a feminism that demands not the restitution of rights or equivalence but instead the end of propriety itself and the infinite indebtedness it incurs. To make a world without debt entails the eviction of propriety as a direct relationship between bearing specific characteristics and a proper way of appearing and being. Here, the work of Verónica Gago (2020) and #NiUnaMenos (Not One More) in Argentina is particularly important. Gago points out how the pressures now exerted on the very intimacies of social life, expressed through variegated household instabilities, reflect both the plundering of public infrastructures and the ways in which the "neighborhood" functions as the locus of not only practical solidarity but also the reproduction of the looting of capacity and resources. New forms of indebtedness, the systematic undermining of stable shelter, the proliferation of home-based work, and the mediations of cheap logistics delivery and administrative platforms shift the terms and terrain of domesticity, of what home means.

Feminism thus operates as raw material in a time of crisis because it situates itself in a double bind where, on the one hand, social care is the only way to navigate plunder but, on the other, care is the very thing being plundered. Feminist mobilizations across massive streets and more intimate neighborhoods are the concretization of a collective inhabitation that belongs to no specific territory, that produces nothing but its own prospective endurance as it secondarily ramifies across different demands—the end of eviction, the enforcement of the criminalization of gender violence, and so forth. But the most important materialization is that feminist mobilization, at least that manifested by the Argentine example, is situated both within and outside the double bind of care.

On the one hand, it is important to revalue the sensibilities, practices, sacrifices, and efforts that constitute the essential work of social reproduction embodied by the female leadership of households. But if the household is to be reproduced and repurposed in its existing logics and forms, regardless of female leadership, is a prospective dissolution of those household forms then a dispossession or necessary transformation of critical sociality? What manifests itself as plunder, as opposed to transformation? How is the very experience of domesticity, intimacy, and social cooperation securitized as rights to the future, and whose rights and whose future?

As the household is crisscrossed by different struggles and different rent-seeking apparatuses, what of the household can be sustained as generative ferment that at least wards off premature enclosure, and what is simply a carceral experience? These are often immediately experienced in the present as undecidable questions, the terms of a debilitating double bind. So feminism is necessarily a collective orientation rather than individual embodiment and articulated as a mobilization of rebellion rather than as a concrete space of inhabitation. But it is uncertain where that rebellion lands.

Technical Accompaniments

What to make of these reflections on rebellion without redemption? My claim is that they are rehearsals for a militant sensibility that takes the world, this world, head-on; that takes the world on by taking it in and being within it in an extensive manner, undaunted by its contradictions or sheer brutality. Of course, where rebellion lands depends on effort, strategy, tactics, context, courage, and luck. Still, this notion of taking it on by multiplying the angles through which we take it in does not mean that we come to understand it any better or are able to bend it to emancipative strivings or the conviction that now everything might be changed. Rather, it is stance aimed at overcoming whatever reticence we might have in deploying the technical tools at our disposal, even as we necessarily must remain wary of their untoward implications. In part this is not only about different kinds of uses but also about different imaginations of the technical.

Here, what I have in mind is the systematicity entailed in the intersections of propinquity, fortuity, abandon, and hard-nosed skill that continuously create operational spaces for the urban dispossessed, forced into one temporary occupation after another. From the composition of Shi'ite shrines in Lahore, with their circuits of provisioning sufficient to sustain the 24/7 collective conversations that take place among thousands of people passing in and out, to the owner of one of the largest computer shops on Mumbai's infamous Lamington Road, who subsidizes airtime for street youths across the city as the elemental infrastructure for his determination to help families locate relatives who have been lost to the city—the technical is a surfeit of unruly sense pieced together in uncommon conjunction of bodies, things, and places. In the 1980s and early 1990s migrants from the Transkei and Zululand moved en masse into the largely Indian neighborhoods of Durban that had been formed through the apartheid Group Areas Acts. Some of the migrants settled on the slopes beneath suburban homes and tapped into electricity lines running into those homes so that they could illuminate their shacks and televisions and watch football games (Pithouse 2008; Chari 2010).

There are spare parts stores in Delhi, filled to the brim with every imaginable item that has been used in any type of electronic equipment for decades and piled along endless and crowded shelves. There are no formal inventories or classification systems, no records or maps indicating precisely where a specific type of item has been lodged. Rather, the staff quickly move through the aisles of circuit boards, monitors, pins, wires, bearings, battery packs, and cartridges according to a calculus that intersects, for example, the fungibility of a part, its capacity to play a role in compositions that differ from its original position, its roundness or flatness, color, and texture, its relative rarity, and its prospects for reuse. All the staff have not only memorized such a calculus but come to intuit it as well. So a working geography here is constituted not by subjecting the details of a particular item to strict classifications of what that item was in the past, but rather by considering what it could be and the apparent likelihood of that disposition.

In other words, there is a tenuous form at work here that enables a sense of continuity, of parts being related to other parts, of parts pointing to each other as potentialities in different virtual assemblages. Yet there is no fixed "body" involved, no strict order of coherence. The array of materials is curated as a speculation, but a speculation that requires a shape, some kind of measure that might indicate how things that are occurring now might be related to things occurring "then." And as some kind of volatile and temporary amalgamation of past and future, there is a "then" that is not specified either way. All these details, these parts, have been somewhere else and carry the effects of their past belongings, now shaken off partly, within a dynamic mode of waiting, waiting to see what might become of them. Customers not privy to the working maps of the staff are equally encouraged to roam around. They may have come in with specific requests, but the encouragement to roam is a lure to see if anything comes to mind, to dream their plans differently and not worry if the risks they take in selecting an item against the grain doesn't work. The owner reassures them that the parts are always returnable, if not at the same price. Customers are encouraged to then pursue idiosyncratic purchases, purchases against the grain, which in turn add new twists and turns to the calculus underlying the store's geography.

That said, the actual present uses of the technical skew in terms of larger projects that curtail the negotiability of dispositions, which renders the future the realization of the most proficient formatting of probabilities. Technicity, as manifested through the hegemonic modes of contemporary calculation, tends to diminish knowledge production and sharing as a critical dimension of collective life. The increasingly automated ways in which futures are specified, incorporated as probabilities into the present, threatens to obviate the need for collectivity. As Bernard Stiegler (2018) emphasizes, the compensation for this wounding of the collective by the technical will necessarily be technical itself, and a matter of invention. If the imagination of a future for the collective can only emanate from the collective itself, we must understand then the nature of such a collective both within and outside the terms of the technical. This necessitates discovering new ways of sharing technical instruments and developing institutions of pedagogy and experimentation that establish cultures of knowledge production capable of effectively mediating the interpenetrations of the technical, collective, and human.

The rationalization of urban inhabitation—subjecting it to a more uniform and transparent series of rules and norms, while at the same time encouraging more individualistic forms of accountability and livelihood—is substantiated with a vast infrastructure of sensors, monitoring, and tracking systems. Stiegler (2009) is right to say that the digital is "above all a process of generalized formalization." Formalization is a process of unification attained through codes and algorithms that affect actions of all kinds, from the use of GPS systems in driving a car to the continuous feedback offered to individual bodies about a wide range of metabolic and psychological functions. Continuous monitoring of bodies in action is manifested in smart phone applications that are able to identify the location of an individual at any time, compulsions to communicate the most mundane events via social media, which are then subjected to an evaluative system of likes and dislikes, and the storage of data and personal communication on cloud structures of uncertain sovereignty, which in turn offer continuous probabilistic weightings of optimal pathways and decisions for individual users to pursue. All these enact an extensive and intensive formalization of the relationships between individuals and the city (Crandall 2010).

Formalization tends to feed forward into the future by preemptively shaping what might be registered as adverse encounters to come. Risk mitigation is predicated not so much on curtailing the event of risk as on actualizing it within the present as a means of mitigating its disruptive force, bringing it to life through a particular way of illuminating a social field (Neyland 2015; Amoore 2019). Here the biographical stories of individuals and the relationships among known social categories are less important than an algorithmically driven scrutiny of diffuse social fields, a scrutiny that looks for particular patterns of unfolding events that are strange or immanently disruptive, and where the subsequent intervention is less a matter of disciplining particular categories of the population and more a matter of the design of built environments, thresholds, interfaces, screens, and trajectories of movement (Pasquale 2015; Vignola 2017; Dieter and Gautier 2019).

In other words, these are interventions into the materiality of encounters, about how to diffuse, absorb, intercept, deflect, and circumscribe. All are techniques for engineering space. Such formalization is predicated on the assumption that it is economically and technically unviable to preclude encounters, to expend resources on keeping people in place, even if social mobility produces a situation where individuals are substantially encumbered with debt, unsustainable levels of personal consumption, and constricted labor markets, all of which introduce inertia. Rather, the prevailing logics of control tend toward conceding the relative inability of institutions to keep people in place—from family, kinship, community, disciplinary, sectoral—and utilize advanced surveillant assemblages to target wayward movements.

Interception can take many forms, ranging from everyday harassment that forces a person to avoid certain areas at certain times, targeted assassinations of "suspected" terrorists, the use of urban designs such as antihomelessness spikes and narrow benches (backed by laws against panhandling), the sudden demolition of "illegal structures" and temporary homes, the use of private security guards, and extensive border patrols. It is designed simply to make particular kinds of movement and inhabitation impossible, and to *shift* problematic populations and practices elsewhere (Valayden 2016).

Ruha Benjamin (2019) has signaled the advent of the "New Jim Code" as the means by which racialism is reformulated through algorithmic computation without the need for race to be enunciated directly. Instead, race is reiterated through a proliferation of ancillary categorizations and niche identifications, as well as through the encoding of race as an apparently neutral attribution, among others. Ramon Amaro's (2019) work on Black facial (mis)recognition emphasizes the extent that computer vision consolidates the myth of individuals constituted on the basis of coherence and categorical division. Artificiality comes to exemplify human reason in such a way that the heterogeneous life experiences of individuals are subsumed as variations of an overarching set of operational logics, specifiable and comparable. "This astonishing circumvention of indeterminacy naturalizes and objectifies the variant ways in which human beings live their lives to a degree that any mode of coexistence becomes no more than a transcendental presence brought forth by a single epistemological point of view."

The profusion of algorithmic calculability will continue unabated, dispersed across more and more aspects of daily life. Concomitantly, personal data continues to be consolidated as the predominant currency enabling a more proficient targeting of rule and population control. Methodologies of detection are more attuned to the finer gradations of life generated by these methodologies themselves. But as Luciana Parisi (2016a, 2016b) points out, programmatic calculation is not simply the execution of instructions but a machine ecology thoroughly infected with randomness. As such, digital infrastructures potentiate unanticipated, sometimes illegible scenarios not easily subsumed by the dictates of techno-capitalism, yet almost always adaptable to them. As soon as actualities come together, as soon as supposedly discrete events and objects feel each other out, are placed in some kind of relationship with each other, are assessed in terms of their impact on each other or their respective genealogies of appearance, no matter how prescriptive or limiting their interactions might be, they always suggest a potential of what might have taken place, of nondenumerable dispositions.

This does not mean that the view onto the world is some uninterrupted smooth and networked space. Frictions, borders, blind spots, and partiality abound. But what is frictional, bordered, or transitional becomes increasingly uncertain. Getting in or being left out, moving from here to there, may remain substantive empirical experiences. But where we may appear, and to whom; what we have access to under specific circumstances; or what side we may occupy in multiple antagonisms makes any assessment of our overall position less clear. This entails not only the familiar processes of hacking or stealth but the strange duplicities that might ensue from the now-normative reference to networked sociality. This is as evident in subaltern as in multi-national corporate domains.

Toward Popular Technicity

I recall stories from Khartoum, when sandstorms, called *haboob*, would often overwhelm the city, turning the sky completely dark at midday and inundating the atmosphere with the finest grained particles that even layer upon layer of covering would be hard-pressed to keep out. Following the haboob, police records would document large numbers of thefts from houses, such as the complete disappearance of furnishings and automobiles that suddenly vanished, leaving no trace. Some households were reluctant to talk about these occurrences, fearing that adverse judgments would be made about their moral stature or sanity; others were overeager to spill the beans, claiming they had lost everything.

Many residents in Khartoum's upscale neighborhoods had used all their resources simply to purchase land and build large edifices in high-status areas; they would then have nothing left with which to populate the interiors. Attributions of such theft could easily be viewed as an excuse for having built beyond one's means. Yet in Haj Yousif, Mayo, and Ombada, the predominant subaltern areas of Dinka, Nuer, Shilluk, and Nuba residency in the city, there is a precise recounting of these disappearances. Waybills are soon displayed about how the loot is already on lorries heading toward South Sudan and maps are drawn to outline the best ways to avoid police roadblocks. Large numbers of residents in these neighborhoods seem to be in possession of the most intimate details concerning the households that have been "appropriated," as if they had been the objects of "stake-outs" for long periods of time.

Verification of these claims is, of course, shrouded in ambiguity, as it is possible to confirm the truth of situations only anecdotally. The only official documentation rests with police records. But this is not the point. For the intertwining of winds, grand theft, extensive distributed knowledge of details, and the coordination of discussions reveals a *collectivity* without specific form, yet capable of a tangible intervention in the city, a momentary reversal of powers. A reversal that is mostly blamed on the wind. What is this attribution of capacity to the physical force of the wind that purportedly enables a collective activation of force among the most marginal of Khartoum's

121

residents? What is this performance of a nearly encyclopedic knowledge of the city's spatial composition and the multitude of itineraries that traverse it? Can it be considered a platform of algorithmic operations? What is this mutual possession of collective capacity and a calculative figuring? What is this way in which a collectivity that cannot be proven to exist hacks into the transversal operations of the city, upends its certainties of property, and produces the possibility that somehow the oppressed are biding their time, holding onto to a critical opacity by which the elite are haunted and to which they are also completely indebted?

The irony of our prevalent relationship to technical operations is that we work them in order to figure out what we think might constitute a deeply felt expression of who we are, as though somehow, technical operations can be made to represent more precisely the singularity of our positions and sentiments. Yet, why do we think that such technicities have anything fundamental to do with us? Why do we think they have to be grounded in our own meanings, when it is their very distance, exteriority, that makes them useful as a way of touching upon things without our perceptions and orientations? When Instagram throws our images and words across an unmonitorable expanse of views and situations, any stability of the performing self is unsettled. Similarly, the aggregation of our personal details could care less about who we are or what we want to be. The algorithms are only interested in our behavior, and identity is functional only as a shifting filing system.

For Sean Cubitt (2020), network subjectivity converts individual persons into conduits of variegated mediatic flows and corporeal responses whose dispositions are held in reserve by data conglomerates. These are to be put to work in redirecting the compositions, intensities, and speeds of subsequent flows. In the face of a permanent dissatisfaction generated by a never-ending appropriation of affect and creativity, the possibilities of self-articulation rest with the proliferation of the hypothetical, of what we *might be right now* in terms of unfolding events and capacities. Here the authentic, the truly felt and embodied, and the fantasy of liberation is displaced by all kinds of scenarios and simultaneously self-effecting and self-effacing maneuvers that disrupt any equivalence between a proper identity and proper behavior. These do not line up and are instead in a relation of mutual accompaniment without obligations or mutual indebtedness.

Here, the technical is always available as a means of opening up the very ways in which human life has been individuated into specific pathways of "making sense" to a larger reserve of immanent potentiality (Lotti 2015). The relations between nature and human life, progressively modified through the detachment of specific forms of valuation from the mutual "give and take" relationality among the human, the inhuman, and the material, and thus linked to a faith in the apparatuses of control, are availed a world of values beyond use and exchange. For as Gilbert Simondon (2015, 515) emphasizes, the value of the dialogue of the individual with the technical object is to preserve human effort and to create a transindividual domain distinct from community, within which the notion of freedom takes sense, that transforms the notion of individual destiny but doesn't crush it. "[The technical being] is the correlative of the individual's autocreation." Simondon (2017, 303) goes on to say:

> The valorization of technical ensembles and their normative value entail a very particular form of respect, which has in view pure technicity in itself. It is this form of respect, founded on the knowledge of technical reality, and not on the prestige of the imagination, which can penetrate culture. A large highway, at the edge of a big city, imposes this form of respect; moreover, a harbor, the rail traffic signal regulation center, or the control tower of an aerodrome impose this same form of respect: the key-points of a network possess this power, insofar as they are key-points, and not because of the direct prestige of the technical objects they contain.

The reimagination of technicity points to a choreography of accompaniments in the mundane everyday scenarios of our built and social environments. Take a scenario from an "ordinary" city: the stoplights adjusted to flows of traffic; the rhythms of use for the car wash that never closes or for the supermarket across the road that keeps similar hours; the schedule of garbage trucks and street cleaning machines; the amalgamations of schedules of people leaving and coming back from work; the daily rituals of storefront shutters being open and closed; the punctuations of police sirens and emergency vehicles; the morning rush to get to school and the lingered exits in the mid-afternoon; the delivery trucks piling up on a single thoroughfare, slowing down the circulation of traffic; the roars from a cafe with a crowd ensconced in front of a televised sport event. All these instances have their parts to play, have more-or-less detailed itineraries of execution. All are also detached from each other as observable events, yet constitute a reality to which all must at least implicitly respond. None is on its own, but neither are they (collectively) a system. Even if one falters or disappears, the performance proceeds, not in the same way, not without the plural accompaniments that each is for the other.

As Erin Manning and Brian Massumi's (2014) investigations of perception and movement have emphasized, every time we perceive something

123

3.2 | Ordinary intersections. Photograph by Michele Lancione.

occurring in an environment, it entails a process of "reciprocal interfusion." Something is apportioned out to us as we apportion ourselves out to it. This is a process of mutual figuring rather than the imposition of our intentions upon the objects or experiences within the environment. This mutual reaching toward a conjoint enactment, which is the basis for perception, is set against a backdrop where there could be many different alternative realizations. Whatever is perceived in the enactment of a relationship between an environment and us is always an instance of some larger potentiality that already exists, not outside the possibility of perception, but that does not require perception in order for it to be present. In other words, a technical operation, a process of something taking form.

Even in the midst of repression and marginalization, this something taking form—not yet formalized—has been a critical feature of Black cognition. The work of Tina Campt (2017, 2019), reiterating Sylvia Wynter's call to take the senses as theoreticians, focuses on the affective possibilities within the tight spaces of the quotidian rather than on their outsides. Her analysis of how ID photos taken of Black individuals under various colonial regimes seem to look beyond any semblance of the present moment unsettles sense and settles it into new formations that have a political charge precisely because they have a subterranean force that travels underneath and through colonial technologies of space and time. The notion of sounding—from raising voices, to call and response, to drummed communiques across plantations, to the aural navigations of desert nomads—has always been at the heart of Black territories of operation. Dhanveer Singh Brar (2020) in his work on the sonic experimentations of Black East and South London, from sound systems and pirate radios to ambient techno and grime, illustrates the ecologies that allow for the sensory production of alternative inhabitations that circumvent the omnipresent violence of racial policing. Similarly, Nettrice Gaskins (2019) assembles an archive of what she deems "techno-vernacular creativity," a way of intersecting art, engineering, and material expropriation in continuous works in progress that actively ambiguate the borders of established practices and identities, so as to stake out Black futures beyond capture. Here the Detroit Digital Stewards Program is particularly salient, as self-sufficient local area networks (LANs) for hyperlocal communication and shared libraries of audio and text resources are established in ways that articulate different forms of sociality.

In Janelle Monae's opening cut, "Dirty Computers," of the album similarly titled, reference is made to Black queer life being the equivalent of a dirty computer whose processor must be wiped out, cleaned, not so much of particular data and files as of the specific ways in which calculations, computing, and processing are actually conducted. The dispositions of such processing may indeed be hard to handle, but what is more dangerous is their capacity to generate outcomes that normative regimes of sense-making and sense-enforcement cannot readily anticipate. For they surface propositions for the world that appear to come from the world in ways that disrupt the ability to know in advance just what exactly that world comprises. This is why Monae talks about being subjected to, made a subject from the erasure of processing, reduced to a body that does not compute. Not dissimilarly, Ravi Sundaram (2015) points out how urban residents in the postcolony, instead of adhering to particular regimes of moral conduct and verification, increasingly produce their own scenarios and evidence through the widespread dissemination of images, texts, and tweets that are aggregated in various forms and targeted for specific purposes and audiences. Irregular vectors of political force are produced through a new *nervous system*: new geographies and velocities of circulation, shifting circuits of cross-purposes, collision and complicity.

Things can touch each other in unprecedented ways, and the process of counting can open up unanticipated uses of these things. As emphasized in the first chapter, how many spaces across urban regions are underused, vacated, provisionally occupied, and in how many ways can their dormancy be re-purposed to provide temporary platforms for the intersections of different activities and the things and resources they have access to? Also, take, for example, the long-existing working districts of central Jakarta, characterized by the intricate cultivation of territories of operation for heterogeneously composed households and their footholds in different, complementary forms of local work. This work includes the collaborative making of the local built environment itself, largely embodied as a *nonproprietary* orientation to the generation and use of resources. Here, transit entails the continuous circulation of people and things through various uses, occupations, and positions.

But these districts now face a host of serious challenges. These include inflated land valuation, cheap imports, changing cultural values, and monopoly capture of local production systems. But through the development of varied low-cost applications that amass back-end data about the hundreds of workshops, thousands of machines, skill levels of workers, and modalities and scales of distribution chains within specific districts, an expansive notion of "inventory" for everyday users is created. Such an inventory potentiates a wide range of collective entrepreneurial operations capable of renewing the economic elasticity and vitality of these districts. These operations coincide with attempts to secure neighborhood-based accords of resource distribution and accountability that attempt to make sense of the aggregated effects of plural data streams. While such local economies remain intensely vulnerable to the whims of global financial maneuvers, they also reflect provisional ways in which continuous hacking into the tools used to control society *maybe* constitutes a means to keep going, of holding onto the trappings of long-honed collective lives.

Something Specific

In this discussion of all the ways the technical acts as a double-edged sword, simultaneously furthering and impeding any enactment of human will and providing multiple new opportunities for collective organization while diminishing the scope of negotiability and indeterminacy, what I emphasize here is the notion of something *specific* being made, being done. The technical is our accompaniment in generating propositions, scenarios, and emplacements that are specific to this world, this time, and not readily translatable or redeemable. Instead of the infinite relationality promised by algorithms, something comes together that refuses the terms of past recognition or valuation, rebels against its meanings and prophecies, yet portends, perhaps even

3.3 | Specific destinations. Photograph by Michele Lancione.

suggests, the look of what is to come. That in the murky relationships between people and technical instruments, as well as in different materialities and nonhuman forms and forces, something *specific*, simultaneously inside and outside, is provisionally established. Provisionally, in that whatever is made specific does not so much seek to institutionalize itself or defend its accomplishments but prepares instead to move on, become something else, which may or may not have something to do with the specificities that have been materialized. The practice of a rebellion through specificity, belonging not to specific individuals, collectives, or technical instruments but rather *in* their arrangements of accompaniment is my final "version" of the surrounds.

An important caveat to be made concerns the ways in which multiple authoritarian narrations act to singularize meaning. Whether this manifests itself in the most simplistic populist messages, the reduction of pluralist perspectives to "fake news" or absolutist ideologies, or constant attributions of conspiracy, such singularities would seem to collapse heterogeneity to an enforced sense of purity. The authoritarian move seeks to undermine the very capacity of multiple specificities to exist and seeks to subsume every possible interpretive act into its terms.

Specificity, in the way I conceive it here, is not to subsume or integrate, not to provide an overarching narrative for all that takes place, but to act

127

as a counterweight to the more facile versions of the sense that anyone can become anything, of the sense of an incessantly malleable social body always in the process of being remade, or of the sense of immanence that implicitly promises enhanced vitality. For, there is something about this sense of being able to be almost anything or of a sociality constantly in the process of becoming that may reiterate the position of the slave. For even bearing the dismissal of being someone fully human, the slave, nevertheless, was seen as being capable of extraordinary power, an inordinate combination of savagery and competence. Despite attributions of lacking intelligence and will, the slave could be possessed and thus possess all the most desired and repressed forces of nature. As Sara-Maria Sorentino (2019, 187) warns: "We need to linger with the hypothesis that the blob of the social, the problems and potentials of use, the virtue of death, the seductions of the prior may all be accretions of the way the timeless slave as an anti-black, ungendered position infects thought, deranges time, delineates death, demarcates human-ness, and disavows its violence. Otherwise, any turn to form-of-life or collective action is always already reproducing the gesture whose neo-Republican root crystalizes the natural slave: All Lives Matter."

Especially in recent times, as the imperative for salvation, unable to express itself in affiliations with well-known religious discourses, seeks refuge in the cosmologies of various indigenous peoples seen as embodying spiritual capacities and natural wisdoms that will rescue humanity from the brink of extinction, the position of the slave is reiterated as that which does the redemptive work for us. As Hortense Spillers (2003) has always repeated, it is not the job of Black people to save white people from themselves. Or, as Austin Lillywhite (2019, 114) astutely observes:

> Echoing earlier modernist instantiations, the posthuman and new materialist desire to get in touch with the radical alterity of primitive others is used as a means to achieve a redemption for the Western self in the midst of the realization of its own banality and self-destructiveness (or "over-mechanization"). Primitivism is born out of the modern self's desire to transform itself, to be reborn in a new flesh. The projected, spectacularized image of the primitive, which attaches to bodies that do not look like one's own, is reclaimed as the inversion of one's own image. It is the desire to see oneself inside out, participate in a self that is its own outside.

Specificity leaves redemption out of the picture. It is on its own, yet never alone, never the only game in town. It doesn't attempt to position itself with others in any comparative gesture. It knows that it has to get along, that it exists within a larger ambit of things. At the same time, it is like that generalized West African Islamic ethos I mentioned in the first chapter, where every person is inscribed in and by a specific project that can only be realized through deterring constant attempts by others to extract from it, to dilute or distort it. Thus, what one performs, in all the different versions of oneself that can be dissimulated on the basis of everything that project is not, is a constantly moving hinge that never stabilizes the lines of sight and exposure. As such, it can be in the world in many different ways but retains its own coherence, simply because no genealogical or political economic analysis can quite catch up to all the ways in which it repeatedly enunciates itself.

Here, I draw upon my many decades working in the rambunctious neighborhoods of many Global Southern cities. Cities like Manila, Bangkok, Jakarta, Lagos, Karachi, and Mexico City function largely through the capacity to suture together intensely discrepant idioms, places, materials, and ways of life into circuits, itineraries, conduits, and transactions. These produce specific atmospheres, socio-spatial arrangements, material capacities and affective zones. But the details can always resist reified or inert configurations; they can always be somewhere else, folded into new games or dispositions and spirals. Yet, each neighborhood, no matter how similarly subjected to the well-worn refrains of autogestion, dispossession, and underdevelopment, register their own unyielding capacities affecting their endurance beyond considerations of locational advantage, political patronage, or even collective personality.

It is true that in these cities, infrastructure is not only material composition but a story or multiple stories proposing how things got to be the way they are, of how different aspects of urban regions are articulated, while at the same time generating differentiation in the very operations of that narrative (Cross 2014; Harvey and Knox 2015). As such, infrastructure marks the subsequent differentiations among the serviced, the un- or underserviced, the complete or incomplete, the workarounds, circumventions, gaps, and closures, and so forth. At the same time, infrastructure is more than representational or machinic. Stephen Graham and Simon Marvin's (2001) notion of *splintering* powerfully captures the disjunctions and inequities of provisioning, the disparate valuations among different ways of articulating and being articulated to urban spaces. It accounts for the ways in which particular logics and materialization of connectivity are converted into financial assets and dispersed governmentality across an often-wide range of shifting compositions. Splintering is also reflected in the ways in which infrastructure is also always already exposed, its surfaces open to both anticipated and unanticipated flows, wearing, tensions, extreme weather, and feedback loops.

129

Vilém Flusser's (2005) well-known phrase, there is a "confusion of cables," refers to the ways in which the bounds and definitions that some infrastructure supposedly sustains are transgressed by the operations of other infrastructure that pump information in and out of discrete homes, workplaces, and institutions. Sometimes it is not clear where infrastructure is going, both sheen and dilapidation acting as a ruse, as some of the most "modern" of projects end up having short lifespans and as near-ruins functionally are operative or repeatedly transformed for foreseeable futures. Yet, there are aspects of *infrastructuring* that would seem more *detached* than *splintered* in that they enable the production of an *intransitive specificity*, an arrangement of capacity and collective sensibility that cannot be translated or articulated into any generalizable terms, that cannot be measured according to scales of efficacy, but that rather just *do what they do*.

Take for example the complexions of the built environments of those seemingly iconic "popular districts" in the Global South I mentioned just before. Typically self- and incrementally built over time, these well-represented urban spaces are replete with a panoply of materials, designs, and reticulations to services, social compositions, and spatial arrangements. It is possible to construct reasonable genealogies of how the apparent "messiness" of these environments got to be the way it is (Jiminez Corsin 2017). Through combining archival work, oral histories, and geomatic tools, the multiplicity of land statuses, material assemblages, political decisions, economic activities, and governance technologies can be intersected to provide a working picture of a district's infrastructural complexion. More granular investigations can reveal the ways in which the built environment reflects multiple antagonisms among aspirations and agendas, with their concomitant political accords and social accommodations. The resultant layers of sedimentation and the aggregations of historical traces combined with present technologies of spatial rule certainly posit what it is that residents and denizens of a particular district are able to do and what it is they think they are able to do.

But the operations of infrastructuring go beyond this genealogical scope to inscribe actors in an ongoing series of interactions, forms of witnessing and gathering, and modes of "being together" that construct a particular kind of exposure to the larger world, that ensconce actors in materialized sensibilities of encounter that are specific to the immediate environs in which they operate (Berlant 2016). The borders between territories constantly shift between administrative designations, zones of social intimacy and emotional attachments, circuits of everyday mobility, and shifting forms of authority. Yet, the intersections among conduits of movement, spaces of relative domesticity, the modulations of public and private interaction, the routines of everyday social reproduction, and the vectors of sensation marked out by the materials and designs of built forms generate a specific orientation and capacity, a specific imprint on the larger urban surrounds. This is neither the only orientation nor the only impact. But it is something *specific*, immeasurable and untranslatable, that infrastructuring makes possible.

Such specificity constitutes another instance of the *material resistance* to the discursive-oriented domains of policy and design that seek to outline *relational frameworks*, which in turn seek to attribute particular values, positions, and measures of efficacy to a particular territory. It doesn't mean that these frameworks are superseded by these specificities, only that another, albeit tacit, dimension of collective agency is materialized. Such specificity of a material resistance can be important in terms of engaging the potential trajectories of territories that otherwise might look similar, be subject to basically the same array of conditions, yet diverge in terms of how they do or do not endure.

Earlier in this chapter, I referred to the material resistances of a social housing project in Jakarta that concretizes an ongoing sense of propositions for coordinated actions that extend in all kinds of directions based on the very arrangements of things in space that also structure the ways in which everything circulates in this context. Before the COVID-19 pandemic set in, I was pursuing tentative explorations of so-called underground railroads in Europe, ways in which banal urban landscapes were being repurposed to house the variegated needs and aspirations of *sans papier* African residents. In another massive social housing project in a European urban location that will remain unnamed, rebellion is expressed in the construction of a built environment that on the one hand resonates with the Black Dadaist assemblages of Noah Purifoy in the California desert and the weirdly constructed village of Kenya in Guinea, home of Sekou Toure's longtime marabout, where deciphering what was home, mosque, market, animal pen, or vegetable garden was almost impossible.

In this European suburb, residents, without discernible forms of deliberation or planning, have managed to convert much of the interior of a twenty-story apartment block of four hundred units, which was rapidly being vacated, into a mélange of work studios, media centers, boxing rings, communal domestic and commercial kitchens, artisanal factories, and computer banks that all crisscross each other in a nearly chaotic fashion. Each function intrudes upon the other while also according the other sufficient space to enable specific jobs to be done by specific people who nevertheless find

131

themselves accompanied by disparate actors and activities in conjunctions that may initially appear to be absurd but that, over time, seem to ward off the kinds of consolidations of turf and propriety that often interrupt collective projects. All this has been done while maintaining a facade of complete normalcy, producing the dissimulated image of another problematic estate riven by racial marginality and religious extremism. Years spent effectively keeping the police out and conducting social work at a designated community center were finally parlayed, according to one resident, Fatima, into something she deems simply as "useful."

Here the specificity of what is constructed is intensely specific. It is hard to imagine what this "project" is, let alone how it could be translated into other settings. It is intransitive in the sense that it goes nowhere, and no one seems interested in conducting a genealogy of how it got to be the way it is, what the criteria of effectiveness might be, or even what value it performs. Fatima simply says, "It does what it does."

I don't what to make too much of this. I don't want to foreclose the possibility of grasping all the intellectual and affective labor that went into taking such massive amounts of material apart, under the radar, and re-piecing the intricate trade-offs, concessions, accommodations, and buy-outs, let alone the design and materialization of a vast interior space behind the enduring facades of individualized apartment units. Conceivably, it is a vast money-laundering project or, equally possible, a strange investment from deep pockets interested in an opaque foothold in a potentially turbulent urban district. Yet, its modus operandi, even if critically important, doesn't address the resultant instantiation of something that rebels against any act of translation. Of course, the materialization of something so hidden is going to be reflected in the economy of how those affiliated with it speak about its purposes and operations. Of course, no one is going to give anything away unless cornered, and it is precisely this complicity of affiliates to carry on with a dissembling of their incapacity, their banal ordinariness, as the marginals they are expected to be that is critical to such rebellion. No one expects this thing to last. It is too labor intensive. Things have to be worked at in order to be maintained. There are no apparent corporate bodies or democratic deliberations. There indeed may be, but again this is the *maybe* of the situation.

It is not that the residents here would not want recognition for their efforts, would not want to be seen to be worthy of inclusion in a broader effort of city-making. It is not that they would refuse a demand for justice, a just accounting of what they have done and could do, of their efforts being considered as valuable as those of anyone else. Here, neither pessimism or hopefulness suffices, for there is no capturing the relations and operations at work, nor their outcomes, interventions, and refusals. What residents insist upon is that something else must accompany anything they offer as comprehensible, translatable. And that accompaniment is a specificity without bounds, that is not a placeholder or compensation, that is not a culmination or even a weak representation of who they are. It and they have simply come to be, at this particular moment, what they are. It is not the only thing. But because this specificity isn't interested in the game of identification or assessment, it will accompany them throughout every instance of what they are and can become.

The prefiguring of abolition, if true to its commitment to changing everything, is in a complicated position. It exists in a time that is not of abolition but neither is it detached from it. It also has to be more than transitional. Though it may offer a window onto what we hope might come, what is struggled for, it must both cover its tracks, throw off the scent, and at the same time also surprise and reassure. In an intellectual era long dominated by notions of fluid, noncontractual sociality and immanent becoming, of new organicities and ecological resilience—now frequently reduced to ideology and algorithmic preemption—there is conversely something critical about the construction of a specificity that is only what it is. Something that accompanies everything else without comparison, without judgment, that implicitly rebels against its own potential attainments, that can't be pinned down, that won't go away, that is its own Black cause, and the cause of blackness without punctuation, authority, or end. A specificity that cannot be pinned down, captured. Maybe.

EXTENSIONS BEYOND VALUE

The notion of the "urban" has long occasioned a wide range of reflections and propositions. There is something massive about its dimensions, not only spatially, as the world is considered largely if not completely urbanized, but in the voluminous array of concerns, imaginations, fears, dreams, and analyses brought to bear under its name. *Urban* has been shorthand for many "delicate" matters, from Black-oriented radio to transgressive lifestyles to the embodiment of iniquity or elitism. It has been construed as the material of the masses, the conversion of individuals into homogenous and featureless entities, just as it has been the locus for intensified individuation exemplified through a profusion of niche markets and idiosyncratic values.

In Jamaican patois, *massive* has two countervailing meanings. On the one hand it means an inordinate lack of sensitivity to the real conditions taking place, a sense of extreme self-inflation beyond reason. On the other, it means a collectivity coming into being without a set form but reflective of a desire for collaboration and mutuality. *Massive urbanization* thus means both the voluminous expansion of speculative accumulation, extraction of land value, and replication of vast inequities and disfunction, *and* the continuous emergence of new forms of urban inhabitation, a constant remaking of the social field by what I have in the past called an urban majority. This majority was never so much a sociological or political entity as it was a manifestation of the possibilities and affordances that urbanization "lends" to inhabitants bearing the structural onus of having to largely make "their own way" in urban life—the poor, working- and lower-middle classes, the marginalized and recalcitrant, the inhabitants of generically "Black cities."

This coming into being has always been subject to discipline, extraction, or exclusion while remaining a work in progress, unsettled. Whatever is done to this coming-into-form is accompanied by an instrumentality that lends it something more than what appears to those apparatuses of control that would seek to diminish it. It doesn't mean that freedom is inevitably in the cards; it doesn't mean that a promised land will be reached. Rather, it means that there are aspects of any such aspiration, materialized and enunciated in specific ways, that will elude both capture and captivation, that will find momentary territories of operation to infect and be infected with new elements, exposures, and opportunities to shape-shift into something else besides, right next to that which is often brutally put down or extruded. This is what is meant by *the surrounds*, a shape-shifting matrix of spaces, times, and practices that exist right now within the turbulent processes of contemporary urbanization. These surrounds provide momentary elisions of prevailing dominations and incubations of unprecedented or unanticipated collective expression and are found when diverging forces and agendas don't quite line up, where countervailing land laws and tenure systems, gaps in jurisdictions, anomalies in regulatory frameworks, and contradictions in political rule have generated strange spaces that either no one pays much attention to or that nobody knows how to deal with. The surrounds are those interstices between the accelerated erasure and constant remaking of built environments and the obdurate remainders of spaces whose functions, appearance, and uses seem not to have changed for many decades.

While clearly a minoritarian position, a space of exception, the surrounds is not simply railroaded and effaced as urban form stretches across ever-vaster landscapes. Rather, what I want to suggest in this formulation is a surrounds that also expands within the extensivity of the urban. Of course, what became clear in the time of the COVID-19 pandemic was the fashion in which the need for rectification and formalization was amplified by the unabated conversion of more and more urban space into logistical nodes and new, completely "smart" cities, and the concomitant erasure of long-existent settlements and local economies. Yet, the massiveness of urban regions, long seen as the very embodiment of chaos and disaster, may be the very thing that provides a kind of "safety net." In many regions, populations are being reshuffled, moved from one area to the other, something that an extensive

135

Extensions beyond Value

landscape of built projects that never really worked has allowed, as buildings are repurposed for other uses and as populations also take advantage of contiguities within these new developments of sub-cities, new industrial zones and logistical centers.

The sheer heterogeneity of developments at all scales, from thousands of small developers to large real estate corporations, have equipped regions with a large number of warehouses, housing estates, mega residential developments, industrial zones, commercial centers, and small enterprise districts that either never got off the ground, or only partially fulfilled their intended functions or desired rates of occupancy, or quickly fell apart. When these "projects" are coupled with large swathes of squatter settlements, temporary migrant housing, and the conversion of older residential neighborhoods into mass boarding houses, it is possible to grasp the extensiveness of a circulating population that anchors residency across multiple tenuous residencies, remains completely unanchored in serial short-term occupancies, or is continuously displaced as a function of different instantiations of urban renewal, the migration of employment opportunities, or the increasingly opportunistic sensibilities of residents themselves. All kinds of discrepant environments become momentary bastions of largely improvised collectivity, where people try to make some functional use of each other without any pretense of long-term commitments. Momentary, sporadic, and makeshift become the defining metaphors of many collective formations. The surrounds thus becomes a more predominant feature of urban life, particularly in the Southern latitudes where these changes are most marked.

Of course, this does not mean that the change of everything, the abolitionist imperative, becomes more imminent. With more and multiple possibilities of figuring that can go any which way, the plurality of the surrounds does not enhance the guarantees. It doesn't mean that the hard slog of painstaking organizing and political education will soon come to an end or that it has lost its viability. Rather, it draws attention to the *ordinariness* of the surrounds, revealing its warp and weft and how it unravels itself across a broader canvas of instantiation.

What to make of all these specificities at hand? There are the Sakanat Banat of Fatih, Istanbul, hostels for single Arab women, which simultaneously function as employment agencies, religious seminaries, brothels, market associations, refugee centers, nodes in a vast circulation of goods and documents, artisanal factories, day care centers, and health clinics. The lines among all of these functions blur, yet without diminishing the competence of anyone. In the Nigerien city of Agadez, one of the key transport nodes for

136

Africans moving toward Europe, scores of women's organizations embodying the fundamental practices of hospitality of the Agadestawa of the indigenous people adopt the migrants as their children, shielding them from the long reach of interdictions and predatory practices. In Abidjan, while men are preoccupied with repeated bouts of internecine political conflict, or luring cash from susceptible Europeans in search of African tastes, or trying to prove themselves as slick entrepreneurs in the overcrowded street economies, networks of women's community learning centers, forged initially as prayer circles, manage an intricate distribution system that identifies and targets young girls exhibiting specific skills to forge ongoing relations with each other in neighborhoods across West Africa, helping them access training, higher education, and business opportunities. These emerging and consolidating relations are sustained through the articulated sales of home-based production organized by learning centers. Again, part gang, part NGO, part religious movement, part chamber of commerce, its specificity rests with a form of gathering and mobilization that largely exists for its own sake.

The surrounds brings to life dimensions of urbanity that exist within its structural ambit and manages to enunciate them differently. It doesn't turn things around or toward specific agendas of progressivity or liberation known in advance; it doesn't necessarily know what it does or who and how many it affects. Yet the city, its peripheries, and hinterlands are affected in ways that exceed the terms of viability and value, where *ain't nobody gonna turn it around.*

137

References

Abourahme, Nasser. 2018. "Of Monsters and Boomerangs: Colonial Returns in the Late Liberal City." *City* 22 (1): 106–15.

Addie, Jean-Paul David, and Roger Keil. 2015. "Real Existing Regionalism: The Region between Talk, Territory and Technology." *International Journal of Urban and Regional Research* 39 (2): 407–17.

Alidou, Ousseina. 2005. *Engaging Modernity: Muslim Women and the Politics of Agency in Postcolonial Niger*. Madison: University of Wisconsin Press.

Allahyari, Morehshin. 2019. "Physical Tactics for a Dying Colonialism: Performance-Lecture at the New Museum." *Medium*, February 28. https://medium.com/@morehshin_87856/physical-tactics-for-digital-colonialism-45e8d3fcb2da.

Alves, Jaime. 2018. *The Anti-Black City: Police Terror and Black Urban Life in Brazil*. Minneapolis: University of Minnesota Press.

Amadu, Malum. 1972. *Amadu's Bundle: Fulani Tales of Love and Djinns*. London: Heinemann.

Amaro, Ramon. n.d. "As If." *E-flux Architecture*. Accessed February 28, 2020. https://www.e-flux.com/architecture/becoming-digital/248073/as-if/.

Amin, Ash. 2016. "On Urban Failure." *Social Research: An International Quarterly* 83 (3): 777–98.

Amoore, Louise. 2018. "Cloud Geographies, Computing, Data, Sovereignty." *Progress in Human Geography* 42 (1): 4–24.

Amoore, Louise. 2019. "Doubt and the Algorithm: On the Partial Accounts of Machine Learning." *Theory, Culture and Society* 36 (6): 147–69.

Amoore, Louise, and Rita Raley. 2017. "Securing with Algorithms: Knowledge, Decision, Sovereignty." *Security Dialogue* 48 (1): 3–10.

Anand, Nikhil, Akhil Gupta, and Hannah Appel, eds. 2018. *The Promise of Infrastructure*. Durham, NC: Duke University Press.

Anderson, Ben. 2015. "Governing Emergencies: The Politics of Delay and the Logic of Response." *Transactions of the Institute of British Geographers* 41 (1): 14–26.

Anderson, Ben. 2017. "Emergency Futures: Exception, Urgency, Interval, Hope. *Sociological Review* 65 (3): 463–77.

Barber, Daniel Colucciello. 2016. "The Creation of Non-Being." *Rhizomes: Cultural Studies in Emerging Knowledge* (29). https://doi.org/10.20415/rhiz /029.

Bayat, Asef. 2013. *Life as Politics: How Ordinary People Change the Middle East.* Stanford, CA: Stanford University Press.

Bear, Laura. 2015. *Navigating Austerity: Currents of Debt along a South Asian River.* Stanford, CA: Stanford University Press.

Bear, Laura. 2017. "Anthropological Futures: For a Critical Political Economy of Capitalist Time." *Social Anthropology* 25 (2): 142–58.

Beller, Jonathan. 2018. *The Message Is Murder: Substrates of Computational Capital.* London: Pluto.

Bencherif, Adib, Aurélie Campana, and Daniel Stockemer. 2020. "Lethal Violence in Civil War: Trends and Micro-Dynamics of Violence in the Northern Mali Conflict (2012–2015)." *Studies in Conflict and Terrorism.* https://doi.org/10 .1080/1057610X.2020.1780028.

Benjamin, Ruha. 2019. *Race after Technology: Abolitionist Tools for the New Jim Code.* London: Polity.

Berlant, Lauren. 2011. *Cruel Optimism.* Durham, NC: Duke University Press.

Berlant, Lauren. 2016. "The Commons: Infrastructures for Troubling Times." *Environment and Planning D: Society and Space* 34 (3): 393–419.

Bhan, Gautam. 2019. "Notes on a Southern Urban Practice." *Environment and Urbanisation* 31 (2): 639–54.

Bledsoe, Adam, and Willie Jamal Wright. 2018. "The Anti-Blackness of Global Capital." *Environment and Planning D: Society and Space* 37 (1): 8–26.

Blundo, Giorgio. 2006. "Dealing with the Local State: The Informal Privatization of Street-Level Bureaucracies in Senegal." *Development and Change* 37 (4): 799–819.

Brachet, Julian. 2018. "Manufacturing Smugglers: From Irregular to Clandestine Mobility in the Sahara." *Annals of the American Academy of Political and Social Science* 676 (1): 16–35.

Brachet, Julian, and Judith Scheele. 2016. "A 'Despicable Shambles': Labour, Property and Status in Faya-Largeau, Northern Chad." *Africa* 86 (1): 122–41.

Brachet, Julian, and Judith Scheele. 2019. "Remoteness Is Power: Disconnection as a Relation in Northern Chad." *Social Anthropology* 27 (2): 156–71.

Brar, Dhanveer Singh. 2020. *Teklife/Ghettoville/Eski: The Sonic Ecologies of Black Music in the Early Twenty-First Century.* London: Goldsmiths Press.

Brenner, Neil. 2019. *New Urban Spaces: Urban Theory and the Scale Question.* Oxford: Oxford University Press.

Brenner, Neil, and Christian Schmid. 2015. "Towards a New Epistemology of the Urban?" *City* 19 (2–3): 151–82.

Brickell, Katherine. 2014. "The Whole World Is Watching: Intimate Geopolitics of Forced Eviction and Women's Activism in Cambodia." *Annals of the Association of American Geographers* 104 (6): 1256–72.

Browne, Simone. 2015. *Dark Matters: On the Surveillance of Blackness*. Durham, NC: Duke University Press.

Caldeira, Teresa P. R. 2012. "Imprinting and Moving Around: New Visibilities and Configurations of Public Space in São Paulo." *Public Culture* 24 (2): 385–419.

Campt, Tina M. 2017. *Listening to Images*. Durham, NC: Duke University Press.

Campt, Tina M. 2019. "The Visual Frequency of Black Life: Love, Labor, and the Practice of Refusal." *Social Text* 37 (3): 25–46.

Carter, J. Kameron. 2019. "Black Malpractice (A Poetics of the Sacred)." *Social Text* 37 (2): 67–107.

Cesafsky, Laura. 2017. "How to Mend a Fragmented City: A Critique of 'Infrastructural Solidarity.'" *International Journal of Urban and Regional Research* 41 (1): 145–61.

Chakrabarty, Dipesh. 2019. "The Planet: An Emergent Humanist Category." *Critical Inquiry* 46 (1): 1–31.

Chari, Sharad. 2010. "State Racism and Biopolitical Struggle: The Evasive Commons in Twentieth-Century Durban, South Africa." *Radical History Review* (108): 73–90.

Chari, Sharad. 2017. "The Blues and the Damned: (Black) Life That Survives Capital and Biopolitics." *Critical African Studies* 9 (2): 152–73.

Citton, Yves. 2014. "Politics as Hypergestural Improvisation in an Age of Mediocrity." In *The Oxford Handbook of Critical Improvisation Studies*, edited by George Lewis and Benjamin Piekut, 160–80. Oxford: Oxford University Press.

Citton, Yves. 2017. *The Ecology of Attention*. Translated by Barnaby Norman. London: Polity.

Clare, Nick, Victoria Habermehl, and Liz Mason-Deese. 2018. "Territories in Contestation: Relational Power in Latin America." *Territory, Politics, Governance* 6 (3): 302–21.

Coelho, Karen, Darshini Mahadevia, and Glyn Williams. 2020. "Outsiders in the Periphery: Studies of the Peripheralisation of Low-Income Housing in Ahmedabad and Chennai, India." *International Journal of Housing Policy* (August). https://doi.org/10.1080/19491247.2020.1785660.

Cohen, Tom. 2016. "Trolling 'Anthropos'—Or, Requiem for a Failed Prosopopoeia." In *Twilight of the Anthropocene Idols*, edited by Tom Cohen, Claire Colebrook, and J. Hans Miller, 20–80. London: Open Humanities Press.

Colebrook, Claire. 2012. "Not Kant, Not Now: Another Sublime." *Speculations* 5: 127–57.

Colebrook, Claire. 2014. *Sex after Life: Essays on Extinction, Volume Two*. Ann Arbor, MI: Open Humanities Press.

Colebrook, Claire. 2019. "A Cut in Relationality." *Angelaki: Journal of Theoretical Humanities* 24 (3): 175–95.

141

Colebrook, Claire. 2020. "The Future Is Already Deterritorialized." In *Deterritorializing the Future: Heritage in, of, and after the Anthropocene*, edited by Rodney Harrison and Colin Sterling, 346–83. London. Open Humanities Press.

Coley, Rob. 2019. "In Defense of 'Noir Theory': Laruelle, Deleuze, and Other Detectives." *Theory, Culture and Society* 37 (3): 123–44.

Coole, Diana, and Samantha Frost, eds. 2010. *New Materialisms: Ontology, Agency, and Politics*. Durham, NC: Duke University Press.

Cooper, Melinda. 2017. *Family Values: Between Neoliberalism and the New Social Conservatism*. Cambridge, MA: MIT Press.

Cornea, Natasha Lee, René Véron, and Anna Zimmer. 2017. "Everyday Governance and Urban Environments: Towards a More Interdisciplinary Urban Political Ecology." *Geography Compass* 11 (4): e12310. https://doi.org/10.1111/gec3.12310.

Crosby, Alexandra, and Jesse Adams Stein. 2020. "Repair." *Environmental Humanities* 12 (1): 179–85.

Cross, Jamie. 2014. *Dream Zones: Anticipating Capitalism and Development in India*. London: Pluto Press.

Cubitt, Sean. 2020. "Limen, Portal, Network Subjectivities." *Parallax* 26 (1): 9–19.

Das, Veena, and Shaline Randeria. 2015. "Politics of the Urban Poor: Aesthetics, Ethics, Volatility, Precarity: An Introduction to Supplement 11." *Current Anthropology* 56 (S11): S3–S14.

Deleuze, Gilles. 1997. *Negotiations 1972–1990*. Translated by Martin Joughin. New York: Columbia University Press.

Deleuze, Gilles, and Félix Guattari. 2013. *A Thousand Plateaus: Capitalism and Schizophrenia*. Translated by Brian Massumi. London: Bloomsbury.

Derrida, Jacques. 2000. "Hospitality." Translated by Barry Stocker with Forbes Morlock. *Angelaki: Journal of the Theoretical Humanities* 5 (3): 3–18.

Dieter, Michael, and David Gauthier. 2019. "On the Politics of Chrono-Design: Capture, Time and the Interface." *Theory, Culture and Society* 36 (2): 61–87.

Diouf, Mamadou. 1996. "Urban Youth and Senegalese Politics: Dakar 1988–1994." *Public Culture* 8 (2): 225–49.

Diouf, Mamadou. 2003. "Engaging Postcolonial Cultures: African Youth and Public Space." *African Studies Review* 46 (2): 1–12.

Diouf, Sylviane. 2014. *Slavery's Exiles: The Story of the American Maroons*. New York: New York University Press.

Doshi, Sapana, and Malini Ranganathan. 2017. "Contesting the Unethical City: Land Dispossession and Corruption Narratives in Urban India." *Annals of the American Association of Geographers* 107 (1): 183–99.

Escobar, Arturo. 2008. *Territories of Difference: Place, Movements, Life, Redes*. Durham, NC: Duke University Press.

Escobar, Arturo. 2019. "Habitability and Design: Radical Interdependence and the Re-Earthing of Cities." *Geoforum* 101: 132–40.

Fanon, Frantz. 2008. *Black Skin, White Masks*. Translated by Charles Lam Markmann. London: Pluto.

Fanon, Frantz. 2011. *The Wretched of the Earth*. Translated by Richard Philcox. New York: Penguin Classics.

Ferreira da Silva, Denise. 2018. "Hacking the Subject: Black Feminism and Refusal beyond the Limits of Critique." *PhiloSOPHIA: A Journal of Continental Feminism* 8 (1): 19–41.

Fischer, Michael M. J. 2018. *Anthropology in the Meantime: Experimental Ethnography, Theory, and Method for the Twenty-First Century*. Durham, NC: Duke University Press.

Flusser, Vilém. 2005. "The City as Wave-Trough in the Image-Flood." Translated by Phil Gochenour. *Critical Inquiry* 31 (2): 320–28.

Foucault, Michel. 1986. *The History of Sexuality*. Vol. 2, *The Use of Pleasure*. Translated by Robert Hurley. London: Penguin.

Foucault, Michel. 2011. *The Courage of Truth (The Government of Self and Others): Lectures at the Collège de France, 1983–1984*. Translated by Graham Burchell. New York: Palgrave Macmillan.

Fredericks, Rosalind. 2014. "Vital Infrastructures of Trash in Dakar." *Comparative Studies of South Asia, Africa and the Middle East* 34 (3): 532–48.

Fredericks, Rosalind. 2018. *Garbage Citizenship: Vital Infrastructures of Labor in Dakar, Senegal*. Durham, NC: Duke University Press.

Furniss, Jamie. 2016. "Postrevolutionary Land Encroachments in Cairo: Rhizomatic Urban Space Making and the Line of Flight from Illegality." *Singapore Journal of Tropical Geography* 37 (3): 310–29.

Gago, Verónica. 2020. *Feminist International: How to Change Everything*. Translated by Liz Mason-Deese. London: Verso.

Galloway, Alexander. 2014. *Laruelle: Against the Digital*. Minneapolis: University of Minnesota Press.

Gaskins, Nettrice. 2019. "Techno-Vernacular Creativity and Innovation across the African Diaspora and Global South." In *Captivating Technology: Race, Carceral Technoscience, and Liberatory Imagination in Everyday Life*, edited by Ruha Benjamin, 252–74. Durham, NC: Duke University Press.

Genet, Jean. 1971. *The Screens*. Translated by Bernard Frechtman. New York: Grove Press.

Gilmore, Ruth Wilson. 2021. *Change Everything: Racial Capitalism and the Case for Abolition*. Chicago: Haymarket Books.

Gordillo, Gaston. 2019. "The Metropolis: The Infrastructure of the Anthropocene." In *Infrastructures, Environment, and Life in the Anthropocene*, edited by Kevin Hetherington, 75–102. Durham, NC: Duke University Press.

Gordon, Lewis. 2010. "Theory in Black: Teleological Suspensions in Philosophy of Culture." *Qui Parle: Critical Humanities and Social Sciences* 18 (2): 193–214.

Gordon, Lewis. 2013. "Race, Theodicy, and the Normative Emancipatory Challenges of Blackness." *South Atlantic Quarterly* 112 (4): 725–36.

Graham, Stephen, and Simon Marvin. 2001. *Splintering Urbanism: Networked Infrastructures, Technological Mobilities and the Urban Condition*. London: Routledge.

143

Graham, Stephen, and Nigel Thrift. 2007. "Out of Order: Understanding Repair and Maintenance." *Theory, Culture and Society* 24 (3): 1–25.

Gregson, Nicky, Mike Crang, and Constantinos C. Antonopoulos. 2017. "Holding Together Logistical Worlds: Friction, Seams and Circulation in the Emerging 'Global Warehouse.'" *Environment and Planning D: Society and Space* 35 (3): 381–98.

Gupta, Akhil. 2012. *Red Tape: Bureaucracy, Structural Violence, and Poverty in India*. Durham, NC: Duke University Press.

Halbert, Ludovic, and Hortense Rouanet. 2014. "Filtering Risk Away: Global Finance Capital, Transcalar Territorial Networks and the (Un)making of City-Regions: Property Development in Bangalore." *Regional Studies* 48 (4): 471–84.

Halbert, Ludovic, and Katia Attuyer. 2016. "Introduction: The Financialisation of Urban Production: Conditions, Mediations and Transformations." *Urban Studies* 53 (7): 1347–61.

Haluk, Markus. 2017. *West Papua Dead or Alive: The Loss of Hopes and Human Rights in Papua*. Jayapura: Deiyai and Honai Center for Humanism and Peace.

Hansen, Mark B. N. 2014. *Feed-Forward: On the Future of Twenty-First-Century Media*. Chicago: University of Chicago Press.

Haraway, Donna J. 2003. *The Companion Species Manifesto: Dogs, People, and Significant Otherness*. Chicago: Prickly Paradigm Press.

Haro, Lia, and Romand Coles. 2019. "Reimagining Fugitive Democracy and Transformative Sanctuary with Black Frontline Communities in the Underground Railroad." *Political Theory* 47 (5): 646–73.

Hartman, Saidiya. 1997. *Scenes of Subjection: Terror, Slavery, and Self-Making in Nineteenth-Century America*. New York: Oxford University Press.

Hartman, Saidiya. 2019. *Wayward Lives, Beautiful Experiments: Intimate Histories of Social Upheaval*. New York: W. W. Norton.

Hartman, Saidiya. n.d. "The Plot of Her Undoing." *Notes on Feminisms*. Feminist Arts Coalition. Accessed May 23, 2020. https://static1.squarespace.com/static/5c805bf0d86cc90a02b81cdc/t/5db8b219a910fa05af05dbf4/1572385305368/NotesOnFeminism-2_SaidiyaHartman.pdf.

Harvey, Penny, and Hannah Knox. 2015. *Roads: An Anthropology of Infrastructure and Expertise*. Ithaca, NY: Cornell University Press.

Heynen, Nik. 2016. "Urban Political Ecology II: The Abolitionist Century." *Progress in Human Geography* 40 (6): 839–45.

Hui, Yuk. 2015. "Towards a Relational Materialism. A Reflection on Language, Relations and the Digital." *Culture and Society* 1 (1): 131–47.

Hui, Yuk. 2018. "On the Soul of Technical Objects: Commentary of Simondon's 'Technics and Eschatology' (1972)." *Theory, Culture and Society* 35 (6): 97–111.

Hull, Matthew. 2012. *The Government of Paper: The Materiality of Bureaucracy in Pakistan*. Berkeley: University of California Press.

Hüsken, Thomas, and Georg Klute. 2015. "Political Orders in the Making: Emerging Forms of Political Organization from Libya to Northern Mali." *African Security* 8 (4): 320–37.

Isin, Engin, and Evelyn Ruppert. 2020. "The Birth of Sensory Power: How a Pandemic Made It Visible." *Big Data and Society* (July). https://doi.org/10.1177/2053951720969208.

Jackson, Michael. 2000. *At Home in the World*. Durham, NC: Duke University Press.

Jackson, Steven J. 2014. "Rethinking Repair." In *Media Technologies: Essays on Communication, Materiality, and Society*, edited by Tarleton Gillespie, Pablo J. Boczkowski, and Kirsten A. Foot, 221–39. Cambridge, MA: MIT Press.

Jackson, Steven J. 2019. "Repair as Transition: Time, Materiality, and Hope." In *Repair Work Ethnographies: Revisiting Breakdown, Relocating Materiality*, edited by Ignaz Strebel, Alain Bovet, and Phillipe Sormani, 337–48. Singapore: Palgrave Macmillan.

Jackson, Zakiyyah Iman. 2015. "Outer Worlds: The Persistence of Race in Movement 'Beyond the Human.'" *GLQ: A Journal of Lesbian and Gay Studies* 21 (2–3): 215–18.

Jackson, Zakiyyah Iman. 2020. *Becoming Human: Matter and Meaning in an Anti-Black World*. New York: New York University Press.

Jensen, Casper Bruun. 2015. Experimenting with Political Materials: Environmental Infrastructures and Ontological Transformations." *Distinktion: Journal of Social Theory* 16 (1): 17–30.

Jensen, Casper Bruun. 2017. "Mekong Scales: Domains, Test Sites, and the Uncommons." *Anthropologica* 59 (2): 204–15.

Jiminez Corsin, Alberto. 2017. "Autoconstruction Redux: The City as Method." *Cultural Anthropology* 32 (3): 450–78.

Joronen, Mikko, and Mitch Rose. 2020. "Vulnerability and Its Politics: Precarity and the Woundedness of Power." *Progress in Human Geography*. https://doi.org/10.1177/0309132520973444.

Keil, R. 2018. "Extended Urbanization, 'Disjunct Fragments' and Global Suburbanisms." *Environment and Planning D: Society and Space* 36 (3): 494–511.

Kemmer, Laura. 2019. "Promissory Things: How Affective Bonds Stretch along a Tramline." *Distinktion: Journal of Social Theory* 20 (1): 58–76.

Kemmer, Laura. 2020. "Free Riding Rio: Protest, Public Transport and the Politics of a Footboard." *City and Society* 32 (1): 157–81.

King, Tiffany Lethabo. 2016. "The Labor of (Re)reading Plantation Landscapes Fungible(ly)." *Antipode* 48 (4): 1022–39.

King, Tiffany Lethabo. 2019. *Black Shoals: Offshore Formations of Black and Native Studies*. Durham, NC: Duke University Press.

Kirksey, Eben. 2012. *Freedom in Entangled Worlds: West Papua in the Architecture of Global Power*. Durham, NC: Duke University Press.

Knox, Hannah. 2017. "Affective Infrastructures and the Political Imagination." *Public Culture* 29 (2): 363–38.

145

Kohn, Eduardo. 2013. *How Forests Think: Toward an Anthropology beyond the Human*. Berkeley: University of California Press.

Konings, Martijn. 2018. *Capital and Time: For a New Critique of Neoliberal Reason*. Stanford, CA: Stanford University Press.

Kundu, Ratoola, and Suchismita Chatterjee. 2020. "Pipe Dreams? Practices of Everyday Governance of Heterogeneous Configurations of Water Supply in Baruipur, a Small Town in India." *Environment and Planning c: Politics and Space* 39 (2): 318–35. https://doi.org/10.1177/2399654420958027.

Kuster, Brigitta. 2017. "Europe's Borders and the Mobile Undercommons." *Texte Zur Kunst* 105 (March). https://www.textezurkunst.de.

Kusumaryati, Veronika. 2020. "*Adat* Institutionalisation, the State and the Quest for Self-Determination in West Papua." *Asia Pacific Journal of Anthropology* 21 (1): 1–16.

Lambert, Michael J. 2016. "Changes: Reflections on Senegalese Youth Political Engagement, 1988–2012." *Africa Today* 63 (2): 33–51.

La Roche, Cheryl Janifer. 2014. *Free Black Communities and the Underground Railroad*. Urbana: University of Illinois Press.

Laruelle, François. 2013. *Philosophy and Non-Philosophy*. Translated by Taylor Adkins. Minneapolis: Univocal.

Leclercq-Vandelannoitte, Aurélie, and Jeremy Aroles. 2020. "Does the End Justify the Means? Information Systems and Control Society in the Age of Pandemics." *European Journal of Information Systems* (October): 746–61. https://doi.org/10.1080/0960085X.2020.1820912.

Lefebvre, Henri. 2014. "Dissolving City, Planetary Metamorphosis." *Environment and Planning D: Society and Space* 32 (2): 203–5. Originally published as "Quand la ville se perd dans une metamorphose planétaire," *Le Monde diplomatique* (May 1989): 16–17; republished in *Manière de voir* 114 (December 2010–January 2011): 20–23.

Lewis, George E. 2007. "Mobilitas Animi: Improvising Technologies, Intending Chance." *Parallax* 13 (4): 108–22.

Lilley, Simon, and Dimitris Papadopoulos. 2014. "Material Returns: Cultures of Valuation, Biofinancialisation, and the Autonomy of Politics." *Sociology* 48 (5): 972–88.

Lillywhite, Austin. 2018. "Is Posthumanism a Primitivism? Networks, Fetishes, and Race." *Diacritics* 46 (3): 100–19.

Lindell, Ilda. 2010. "Informality and Collective Organizing: Identities, Alliances and Transnational Activism in Africa." *Third World Quarterly* 31 (2): 207–22.

Lotti, Laura. 2015. "'Making Sense of Power': Repurposing Gilbert Simondon's Philosophy of Individuation for a Mechanist Approach to Capitalism (by Way of François Laurelle)." *Platform: Journal of Media and Communication* 6: 22–33.

MacLeod, Jason. 2015. "From the Mountains and Jungles to the Villages and Streets: Transitions from Violent to Nonviolent Resistance in West Papua."

146

In *Civil Resistance and Conflict Transformation: Transitions from Armed to Nonviolent Struggle*, edited by Veronique Dudouet, 45–76. New York: Routledge.

Mahon, Rianne, and Laura Macdonald. 2010. "Anti-poverty Politics in Toronto and Mexico City." *Geoforum* 41 (2): 209–17.

Manning, Erin, and Brian Massumi. 2014. *Thought in the Act: Passages in the Ecology of Experience*. Minneapolis: University of Minnesota Press.

Marriott, David. 2011. "Inventions of Existence: Sylvia Wynter, Frantz Fanon, Sociogeny and 'the Damned.'" *New Centennial Review* 11 (3): 45–89.

Marriott, David. 2018. *Whither Fanon? Studies in the Blackness of Being*. Stanford, CA: Stanford University Press.

Martin, Craig. 2012. "Desperate Mobilities: Logistics, Security and the Extra-Logistical Knowledge of 'Appropriation.'" *Geopolitics* 17 (2): 355–76.

Massey, Doreen. 2005. *For Space*. London: Sage.

Massumi, Brian. 2014. *The Power at the End of the Economy*. Durham, NC: Duke University Press.

Massumi, Brian. 2017. "Virtual Ecology and the Question of Value." In *General Ecology: The New Ecological Paradigm*, edited by Eric Hörl and James Edward Burton, 345–74. London: Bloomsbury.

Mbembe, Achille. 2013. *Critique of Black Reason*. Translated by Laurent Dubois. Durham, NC: Duke University Press.

Mbembe, Achille. 2019. "Bodies as Borders." *From the European South* 4: 5–19.

McFarlane, Colin. 2007. "Urban Shadows: Materiality, the 'Southern City' and Urban Theory." *Geography Compass* 2 (2): 340–58.

M'charek, Amade. 2013. "Beyond Fact or Fiction: On the Materiality of Race in Practice." *Cultural Anthropology* 28 (3): 420–42.

M'charek, Amade. 2020. "Tentacular Faces: Race and the Return of the Phenotype in Forensic Identification." *American Anthropologist* 122 (2): 369–80.

McKittrick, Katherine. 2006. *Demonic Grounds: Black Women and the Cartographies of Struggle*. Minneapolis: University of Minnesota Press.

McKittrick, Katherine. 2013. "Plantation Futures." *Small Axe* 17 (3): 1–15.

McKittrick, Katherine. 2021. *Dear Science and Other Stories*. Durham, NC: Duke University Press.

McLaren, Duncan P. 2018. "In a Broken World: Towards an Ethics of Repair in the Anthropocene." *Anthropocene Review* 5 (2): 136–54.

Meillassoux, Quentin. 2011. "History and Event in Alain Badiou." *Parrhesia* 12: 1–11.

Melchor, Fernanda. 2020. *Hurricane Season*. New York: New Directions.

Mezzadra, Sandro. 2019. "Forces and Forms: Governmentality and *Bios* in the Time of Global Capital." *positions* 27 (1): 145–58.

Mitropoulos, Angela. 2012. "Uncanny Robots and Affective Labour in the Oikonomia." *Cultural Studies Review* 18 (1): 153–73.

Mitropoulos, Angela. 2019. "New Concepts for Materialism." *Philosophy Today* 63 (4): 1025–36.

Monte-Mór, Roberto L. 2018. "Urbanisation, Sustainability and Development: Contemporary Complexities and Diversities in the Production of Urban Space." In *Emerging Urban Spaces*, edited by Philipp Horn, Alfaro d'Alencon Paula, and Ana Duarte Cardoso, 201–16. Cham, Switzerland: Springer International.

Moten, Fred. 2017. *Black and Blur*. Durham, NC: Duke University Press.

Moten, Fred. 2018. *Stolen Life*. Durham, NC: Duke University Press.

Naas, Michael. 2015. *The End of the World and Other Teachable Moments: Jacques Derrida's Final Seminar*. New York: Fordham University Press.

Nancy, Jean-Luc. 2016. *The Disavowed Community*. Translated by Philip Armstrong. New York: Fordham University Press.

Neilson, Brett. 2012. "Five Theses on Understanding Logistics as Power." *Distinktion: Journal of Social Theory* 13 (3): 323–40.

Neyland, Daniel. 2015. "On Organizing Algorithms." *Theory, Culture and Society* 32 (1): 119–32.

Neyrat, Frédéric. 2018. *The Unconstructable Earth: An Ecology of Separation*. Translated by Drew S. Burk. New York: Fordham University Press.

Ojo, John Sunday. 2020. "Governing 'Ungoverned Spaces' in the Foliage of Conspiracy: Toward (Re)ordering Terrorism, from Boko Haram Insurgency, Fulani Militancy to Banditry in Northern Nigeria." *African Security* 13 (1): 77–110.

Papadopoulos, Dimitris. 2018. *Experimental Practice: Technoscience, Alterontologies, and More-Than-Social Movements*. Durham, NC: Duke University Press.

Parisi, Luciana. 2013. *Contagious Architecture, Computation, Aesthetics, and Space*. Cambridge, MA: MIT Press.

Parisi, Luciana. 2016a. "Automated Thinking and the Limits of Reason." *Cultural Studies ↔ Critical Methodologies* 16 (5): 471–81.

Parisi, Luciana. 2016b. "Instrumental Reason, Algorithmic Capitalism, and the Incomputable." *Multitudes* 62 (1): 98–109.

Pasquale, Frank. 2015. *The Black Box Society: The Secret Algorithms That Control Money and Information*. Cambridge, MA: Harvard University Press.

Patterson, Orlando. 2018. *Slavery and Social Death*. Cambridge, MA: Harvard University Press. First published 1982.

Peano, Irene. 2016. "Emergenc(i)es in the Fields: Affective Composition and Counter-Camps against the Exploitation of Migrant Farm Labour in Italy." In *Impulse to Act: A New Anthropology of Resistance and Social Justice*, edited by Othon Alexandrakis, 63–88. Bloomington: Indiana University Press.

Peano, Irene. 2017. "Global Care-Commodity Chains: Labour Re/production and Agribusiness in the District of Foggia, Southeastern Italy." *Sociologia del Lavoro* 146 (2): 24–39.

Pellizzoni, Luigi. 2020. "The Environmental State between Pre-emption and Inoperosity." *Environmental Politics* 29 (1): 76–95.

Pithouse, Richard. 2008. "A Politics of the Poor: Shack Dwellers' Struggles in Durban." *Journal of Asian and African Studies* 43 (1): 63–94.

148

Povinelli, Elizabeth A. 2012. "The Will to Be Otherwise/The Effort of Endurance." *South Atlantic Quarterly* 111 (3): 453–75.

Povinelli, Elizabeth A. 2016. *Geontologies: A Requiem to Late Liberalism*. Durham, NC: Duke University Press.

Raffestin, Claude. 2012. "Space, Territory, and Territoriality." *Environment and Planning D: Society and Space* 30 (1): 121–41.

Raineri, Luca, and Francesco Strazzari. 2015. "State, Secession, and Jihad: The Micropolitical Economy of Conflict in Northern Mali." *African Security* 8 (4): 249–71.

Retaillé, Olivier, and Olivier Walther. 2012. "Ways of Conceptualizing Space and Mobility: Lessons from the Sahel to the Globalized World." CEPS/INSTEAD Working Paper, no. 2012-24 (May), CEPS/INSTEAD, Luxembourg. https://liser.elsevierpure.com/ws/portalfiles/portal/11782140/Working+Paper+n%C2%B02012-24.

Ribot, Jesse, Papa Faye, and Matthew D. Turner. 2020. "Climate of Anxiety in the Sahel: Emigration in Xenophobic Times." *Public Culture* 32 (1): 45–75.

Rossiter, Ned. 2014. "Logistical Worlds." *Cultural Studies Review* 20 (1): 53–76.

Sadowski, Jathan. 2020. *Too Smart: How Digital Capitalism Is Extracting Data, Controlling Our Lives, and Taking Over the World*. Cambridge, MA: MIT Press.

Samson, Melanie. 2015. "Accumulation by Dispossession and the Informal Economy—Struggles over Knowledge, Being and Waste at a Soweto Garbage Dump." *Environment and Planning D: Society and Space* 33 (5): 813–30.

Savransky, Martin. 2016. "Modes of Mattering: Barad, Whitehead, and Societies." *Rhizomes: Cultural Studies in Emerging Knowledge* (30). https://doi.org/10.20415/rhiz/030.e08.

Scheele, Judith. 2018. "Ravens Reconsidered: Raiding and Theft among Tubu-Speakers in Northern Chad." *African Studies Review* 61 (3): 135–55.

Schmid, Christian. 2018. "Journeys through Planetary Urbanization: Decentering Perspectives on the Urban." *Environment and Planning D: Society and Space* 36 (3): 591–610.

Serres, Michel. 1997. *Genesis: Studies in Literature and Science*. Translated by Geneviève James and James Nielson. Ann Arbor: University of Michigan Press.

Serres, Michel. 2016. *The Five Senses: A Philosophy of Mingled Bodies*. Translated by Margaret Sankey and Peter Cowley. London: Bloomsbury.

Shaviro, Steven. 2003. *Connected, or What It Means to Live in the Network Society*. Minneapolis: University of Minnesota Press.

Simon, Julien. 2011. "The Sahel as a Drug Transit Zone: Actors and Political Consequences." *Hérodote* 142 (3): 125–42.

Simondon, Gilbert. 2005. *L'individuation a là lumière des notions de forme et d'information*. Grenoble: J. Millon.

Simondon, Gilbert. 2017. *On the Mode of Existence of Technical Objects*. Translated by Cecile Malaspina and John Rogove. Minneapolis: Univocal.

Simone, AbdouMaliq. 2014. *Jakarta: Keeping the City Near*. Minneapolis: University of Minnesota Press.

Simone, AbdouMaliq. 2018. *Improvised Lives: Rhythms of Endurance in an Urban South*. London: Polity.

Slama, Marta, and Jenny Munro, eds. 2015. *From "Stone Age" to "Real Time": Exploring Papuan Temporalities, Mobilities and Religiosities*. Canberra: Australian National University Press.

Sorentino, Sara-Maria. 2019. "Natural Slavery, Real Abstraction, and the Virtuality of Anti-Blackness." *Theory and Event* 22 (3): 630–67.

Spillers, Hortense J. 1987. "Mama's Baby, Papa's Maybe: An American Grammar Book." *Diacritics* 17 (2): 64–81.

Spillers, Hortense J. 2003. *Black, White, and in Color: Essays on American Literature and Culture*. Chicago: University of Chicago Press.

Stengers, Isabelle. 2005. "Introductory Notes on an Ecology of Practices." *Cultural Studies Review* 11 (1): 183–96.

Stiegler, Bernard. 1998. *Technics and Time, 1: The Fault of Epimetheus*. Translated by Richard Beardsworth. Stanford, CA: Stanford University Press.

Stiegler, Bernard. 2009. *Technics and Time, 2: Disorientation*. Translated by Stephen Barker. Stanford, CA: Stanford University Press.

Stiegler, Bernard. 2010a. *Taking Care of Youth and the Generations*. Translated by Stephen Barker. Stanford, CA: Stanford University Press.

Stiegler, Bernard. 2010b. *Technics and Time, 3: Cinematic Time and the Question of Malaise*. Translated by Stephen Barker. Stanford, CA: Stanford University Press.

Stiegler, Bernard. 2018. *The Neganthropocene*. London: Open Humanities Press.

Strathern, Marilyn. 1991. *Partial Connections*. Lanham, MD: Rowman and Littlefield.

Suaib, Hermanto, and Anwar Fitriano. 2015. "A Study of Economic Empowerment of Moi Tribe in Sorong, West Papau." *International Journal of Asian Social Science* 5 (12): 694–705.

Sundaram, Ravi. 2015. "Post-Postcolonial Sensory Infrastructure." *eflux* 64 (April). http://www.e-flux.com/journal/post-postcolonial-sensory-infrastructure/.

Surya, Yuyun. 2016. "'The Blacks of Indonesia': The Articulation of Papuan Ethnic Identity on Social Media." *Media and Jornalismo* 16 (29): 93–110.

Syailendra, Emirza Adi. 2016. "Inside Papua: The Police Force as Counterinsurgents in Post-*Reformasi* Indonesia." *Indonesia* 102: 57–83.

Tadiar, Neferti X. M. 2022. *Remaindered Life*. Durham, NC: Duke University Press.

Terrefe, Selamawit D. 2018. "Speaking the Hieroglyph." *Theory and Event* 21 (1): 124–47.

Thomas, Deborah. 2016. "Time and the Otherwise: Plantations, Garrisons and Being Human in the Caribbean." *Anthropological Theory* 16 (2–3): 177–200.

Thomas, Deborah. 2019. *Political Life in Wake of the Plantation: Sovereignty, Witnessing, Repair*. Durham, NC: Duke University Press.

Times of India. 2020. "With No Transport, Migrants Make the Long March Home." *Times of India*, March 27. https://timesofindia.indiatimes.com

/india/with-no-transport-migrants-make-the-long-march-home/articleshow
/74838123.cms.

Tirtosudarmo, Riwanto. 2018. *The Politics of Migration in Indonesia and Beyond*.
Singapore: Springer.

Turner, Matthew D., Augustine A. Ayantunde, Kristen P. Patterson, and E. Daniel
Patterson III. 2011. "Livelihood Transitions and the Changing Nature of
Farmer-Herder Conflict in Sahelian West Africa." *Journal of Development
Studies* 47 (2): 183–206.

Valayden, Diren. 2016. "Racial Feralization: Targeting Race in an Era of 'Planetary
Urbanization.'" *Theory, Culture and Society* 33 (7–8): 159–82.

Viartasiwi, Nino. 2018. "The Politics of History in West Papua–Indonesia Conflict." *Asian Journal of Political Science* 26 (1): 141–59.

Vignola, Paolo. 2017. "Symptomatology of Collective Knowledge and the Social to
Come." *Parallax* 23 (2): 184–201.

Warburg, Anna Braemer, and Stephen Jensen. 2018. "Policing the War on Drugs
and the Transformation of Urban Space in Manila." *Environment and Planning D: Society and Space* 38 (3): 399–416.

Webb-Gannon, Cammi, Michael Webb, and Gabriel Solis. 2018. "The 'Black Pacific' and Decolonisation in Melanesia: Performing Negritude and Indigeni-
tude." *Journal of the Polynesian Society* 127 (2): 177–206.

Weheliye, Alexander G. 2014. *Habeas Viscus: Racializing Assemblages, Biopolitics,
and Black Feminist Theories of the Human*. Durham, NC: Duke University
Press.

Whitehead, Colson. 2016. *The Underground Railroad*. New York: Little, Brown.

Wright, Michelle. 2015. *Physics of Blackness: Beyond the Middle Passage Epistemology*. Minneapolis: University of Minnesota Press.

Wynter, Sylvia. 2003. "Unsettling the Coloniality of Being/Power/Truth/Freedom:
Towards the Human, after Man, Its Overrepresentation—An Argument." *CR:
The New Centennial Review* 3 (3): 257–337.

Zeiderman, Austin. 2016. "Submergence: Precarious Politics in Colombia's Future
Port-City." *Antipode* 48 (3): 809–31.

Index

Page numbers in italics refer to figures.

156

Index

157

urbanization, viii, 4, 17, 34, 40; Black
critical thought and, 13–14; in Conakry, 46–47; extensivity of, vii, ix, 6, 16,
24, 33, 135; massive, 134; multiplicity
of, 25; surrounds and, 9, 13, 32, 101, 135

value, 4, 12, 83–84, 123, 134, 137; actual
or potential, 64, 77; of goods and services, 76; surplus, 16, 33
violence, 50, 63, 91, 116, 125, 128; the
Bloods and, 75; in fictional stories,
113–14; sexual, 106
vulnerability, 19, 53, 78, 98, 99, 106, 109

waste work, 94–95
"we," invocation of, 16, 17, 38, 70
West Africa/Africans, 43–46, 73, 129, 137.
    See also Guinea

West Bengal, 84
Western Europe, 48, 50–51
West Papua, 61–62
Whitehead, Colson, 48–49
whiteness/white people, 48, 90, 91,
    128
wholesalers, 73, 75, 85
women, 136–37; feminism, 115–16; in *Les
Saignantes* (2005), 106–7; time of,
66–67, 104–6, 112, 114–15
world, this, 17, 25–28, 29, 37, 87, 92;
"thisness" of, 81, 101; wretchedness
of, 113
wretched, the, 58–60, 66, 90, 91; in
fictional stories, 111–12, 113
Wynter, Sylvia, 124

youths, 8, 94–95, 96, 106, 117

www.ingramcontent.com/pod-product-compliance
Lightning Source LLC
Chambersburg PA
CBHW050653270326
41927CB00012B/3004